AF757111

'*Ethical Foundations and Guidelines in Islāmic Psychology* is a groundbreaking work that integrates the ethical traditions of Islam with contemporary psychological practice. It is a part of the Focus Series on Islāmic Psychology and Psychotherapy. The book is rooted in the Qur'ān and Sunnah, and offers a comprehensive exploration of core ethical principles, providing invaluable guidance for Islāmic therapists, counsellors, and academics. It examines crucial topics such as moral development, cultural competence, therapeutic integrity, and social justice, making it a vital resource for those seeking to align their psychological practice with Islāmic values. This book serves as both a theoretical foundation and a practical guide. A must-read for anyone invested in the intersection of faith and psychology, it illuminates a path toward ethically sound and spiritually enriched mental health care.'

Professor Dr G. Hussein Rassool, *Professor of Islāmic Psychology, Centre for Islāmic Studies & Civilisations, Charles Sturt University, Australia*

Ethical Foundations and Guidelines in Islāmic Psychology

This book provides theoretical foundations and practical guidelines for an ethically competent integration of Islam and mental health practice.

This book starts with a foundational introduction to the interface between Islam as a religion and mental health practice. It provides a summary of the ethical challenges and concerns raised in mainstream psychological literature and along with a set of Islamically informed ethical guidelines for the integration of Islam and mental health practice. Taking into account the richness of the Islāmic tradition and the nuances of the Islāmic and Muslim cultures, these guidelines will include both general principles and specific considerations. This book concludes by exploring Islāmic ethics outside of the therapy room in relation to research and social justice.

Filling a critical void in both Islāmic mental health literature and ethics literatures, this text provides mental health practitioners, instructors and researchers, and students worldwide with the tools for an ethical integration of Islam within mental health practices.

AbdulGafar O. Fahm is Reader in the Department of Religions at the University of Ilorin, Nigeria, specialising in Islāmic studies. He holds a PhD in Islāmic spirituality and contemporary society from the International Islāmic University Malaysia. His research focuses on Islāmic ethics, spirituality, and civilisation. He has authored numerous scholarly articles on religion, ethics, and socio-spiritual issues. A recipient of multiple academic awards, he is an active member of several professional societies, including the American Psychological Association. His work bridges Islāmic thought and modern ethical challenges, offering insights into contemporary psychological discourse.

Focus Series on Islāmic Psychology and Psychotherapy
Series Editor: Professor Dr. G. Hussein Rassool, Professor of Islāmic Psychology.

About the Series

In contemporary times, there is increasing focus on the need to adapt approaches of psychology, counselling psychology and psychotherapy to accommodate the integration of spirituality and psychology. With the increasing focus on the need to meet the wholistic needs of Muslims, there was a call to adapt approaches to the understanding of behaviour and experiences from an Islāmic epistemological and ontological worldview.

The aim of the Focus Series on Islāmic psychology and psychotherapy is to introduce a range of educational, clinical and research interventions relating to Islāmic psychology and psychotherapy that are authentic, practical, concise, and based on cutting-edge research. Each volume focuses on a particular aspect of Islāmic psychology and psychotherapy, its application with a specific client group, a particular methodology or approach, or a critical analysis of existing and emergent theoretical and historical ideas.

Each book in the Focus Series is written, in accessible language, with the assumption that the readers have no prior knowledge of Islāmic psychology and psychotherapy.

Treating Addiction from an Islāmic Psychology Perspective
G. Hussein Rassool

Spiritual Integration in Islāmic Psychotherapy
Unveiling the Therapist's Soul
G. Hussein Rassool

Quranic Concepts in Islāmic Psychology and Spirituality
Application in the Modern World
Zuleyha Keskin

Ethical Foundations and Guidelines in Islāmic Psychology
AbdulGafar O. Fahm

Ethical Foundations and Guidelines in Islāmic Psychology

AbdulGafar O. Fahm

Routledge
Taylor & Francis Group
LONDON AND NEW YORK

First published 2025
by Routledge
4 Park Square, Milton Park, Abingdon, Oxon OX14 4RN

and by Routledge
605 Third Avenue, New York, NY 10158

Routledge is an imprint of the Taylor & Francis Group, an informa business

© 2025 AbdulGafar O. Fahm

The right of Author to be identified as author of this work has been asserted in accordance with sections 77 and 78 of the Copyright, Designs and Patents Act 1988.

All rights reserved. No part of this book may be reprinted or reproduced or utilised in any form or by any electronic, mechanical, or other means, now known or hereafter invented, including photocopying and recording, or in any information storage or retrieval system, without permission in writing from the publishers.

Trademark notice: Product or corporate names may be trademarks or registered trademarks, and are used only for identification and explanation without intent to infringe.

British Library Cataloguing-in-Publication Data
A catalogue record for this book is available from the British Library

ISBN: 978-1-032-65734-9 (hbk)
ISBN: 978-1-032-65878-0 (pbk)
ISBN: 978-1-032-65885-8 (ebk)

DOI: 10.4324/9781032658858

Typeset in Times New Roman
by Apex CoVantage, LLC

Contents

1 Introduction

In the contemporary world, where faith and psychology are becoming increasingly relevant, the field of Islāmic psychology emerges as a profound discourse that amalgamates spiritual principles with understanding the human psyche. This book, *Ethical Foundations and Guidelines in Islāmic Psychology*, explores the core principles underpinning Islāmic ethics in psychology. The exploration is structured into three integral parts: Foundations of Islāmic Ethics, Applying Islāmic Ethics in Psychological Practice, and Contemporary Issues in Islāmic Ethics and Psychology. Before considering these, exploring Islāmic ethics as a concept is crucial.

1.1 What Is Islāmic Ethics, and What Does It Constitute?

Islāmic ethics, a branch of moral philosophy, encompasses the principles, values, and guidelines derived from the Islāmic religious tradition. It serves as a framework for Muslims, offering insights into what is morally right or wrong and guiding personal and social conduct. Islām ethics is predicated upon several principles, chief among which is the principle of *Tawhîd*. *Tawhîd* emphasises the absolute unity and oneness of God. Central to Islāmic belief is the conviction that God is the ultimate source of moral values, with humans entrusted with the responsibility to heed His guidance. This is evidenced by the countless verses of the Qur'ân (Islām's Noble Book) that enjoin and command Muslims to act based on key ethical principles such as justice, compassion, honesty, humility, and fairness.

The principles of Islāmic ethics are deeply rooted in the Qur'ân and the *Sunnah* (the teachings and practices of Prophet Muhammad [ﷺ]). These principles find their basis in specific commandments, principles, and stories (from the Qur'ân and Hadīth) that impart moral lessons. The Qur'ân serves as the primary source of guidance for Muslims, providing a comprehensive ethical framework that addresses individual conduct, societal relationships, and the broader cosmic order. The Hadīth and the *Sunnah*, based on the actions and sayings of the Prophet (ﷺ), offer practical guidance that can be applied to resolving real-world issues.

DOI: 10.4324/9781032658858-1

Leveraging both, Islāmic ethics underscore the significance of cultivating good character and fostering virtues such as patience, gratitude, and forgiveness. In various Qur'ân verses and Hadīths, Muslims are enjoined to approach their interactions with others with justice and fairness, extend compassion and kindness to those in need, speak the truth always, and manifest humility in their actions. Qur'ân (16:90), for instance, emphasises the importance of justice and ethics, stating:

إن الله يأمركم بالعدل والإحسان وإيتاء ذي القربى وينهى عن الفحشاء والمنكر والبغي

Indeed, Allāh orders justice and good conduct and giving to relatives and forbids immorality and bad conduct and oppression.

To contextualise what it means to do good and forbid evil, Qur'ân (33:21) highlights the exemplary character of Prophet Muhammad (ﷺ), emphasising his ethical behaviour as a model for believers. Various Hadīths of the Prophet (ﷺ) also stress key moral values such as honesty and kindness, reinforcing the ethical fabric of Islām. For instance, the Hadīth of Jibrīl (Angel Gabriel) elucidates ethical values, including the principles of the five pillars of Islām and the concept of *Ihsân* (excellence in worship and ethics). These Islāmic principles, derived from the concept of *Tawhîd*, provide a foundational basis for ethical decision-making across diverse spheres of life, including personal relationships, business transactions, and governance and social interactions. Each sphere of life, alongside corresponding dictates of Islāmic ethics, is considered below.

In personal relationships, Islāmic ethics state the importance of maintaining strong family ties, respecting parents and elders, and treating spouses with kindness and fairness (Zuhaili, 1985). The Qur'ân contains numerous verses emphasising the importance of family ties and respect for parents and elders. Key verses include:

- Surah Al-Baqarah (Qur'ân 2:83):

  وإذ أخذنا ميثق بني إسرائيل لا تعبدون إلا الله وبالوالدين إحسانا وذي القربى واليتامى والمساكين

  And [recall] when We took the covenant from the Children of Israel, [enjoining upon them], 'Do not worship except Allāh; and to parents, do good and to relatives, orphans, and the needy.

- Surah Al-Ankabut (Qur'ân 29:8):

  ووصينا الإنسان بوالديه حسنا وإن جاهداك لتشرك بي ما ليس لك به علم فلا تطعهما

And We have enjoined upon man goodness to parents. But if they endeavour to make you associate with Me that of which you have no knowledge, do not obey them.

Furthermore, Islāmic scholars such as Imām Al-Ghazālī, Imām Ibn Qudāmah, and Imām Ibn Hazm have written extensively on ethics and family relationships in Islām. For example, Imām Al-Ghazālī's book *Ihyā' 'Ulūm al-Dīn* contains a section on social ethics and offers guidance on family relationships. Muslims are encouraged to foster love, care, and support within their families and prioritise the well-being and happiness of their loved ones.

In business and commerce, Islāmic ethics provide guidelines for conducting transactions justly and reasonably (Askari et al., 2014; Chapra, 2016; Khan, 1992). Muslims are encouraged to be honest and transparent in their dealings, to fulfil their contractual obligations, and to avoid engaging in fraudulent practices or exploitative behaviour. As such, Islāmic finance, which adheres to ethical principles such as the prohibition of interest (*ribā*) and excessive uncertainty (*gharar*), has gained significant attention and traction in recent years as a valuable alternative to conventional banking and finance.

Regarding governance and public affairs, Islāmic ethics emphasise the importance of justice, accountability, and the protection of human rights (Davari, 2004; Mahallati, 2016; Tibi, 2017). Islāmic law (Shari'ah) provides a comprehensive framework for governance. It seeks to promote justice, maintain social harmony, and protect the rights of individuals and communities. Muslim rulers and leaders are expected to rule with justice, fairness, and compassion and uphold the principles of Islāmic ethics in their decision-making.

Social interactions are also guided by Islāmic ethics, which encourage Muslims to be kind, charitable, and inclusive in their interactions with others. Islām strongly emphasises the concept of brotherhood and sisterhood, encouraging Muslims to care for one another, support those in need, and foster a sense of community and solidarity. Acts of charity (*zakāt*) and voluntary service (*sadaqah*) are highly valued in Islām, as they promote social welfare and alleviate the suffering of the less fortunate. Islāmic ethics also extend to environmental stewardship and the preservation of natural resources (Benthall, 2003; Foltz, 2003; Pusch, 2016). Muslims are encouraged to be mindful of their responsibilities as custodians of the Earth and to avoid wastefulness, pollution, and the depletion of natural resources. The Qur'ân teaches that the Earth has been created to sustain humanity; Muslims are, therefore, called upon to care for the environment and maintain a balance between their needs and the preservation of nature.

From the foregoing, it is clear that Islāmic ethics provide a comprehensive framework for moral conduct in all spheres of life. Nonetheless, applying this framework can vary across cultural and societal contexts (El-Rouayheb & Schmidtke, 2016; Nuriz & Awang, n.d.). As new issues and perspectives emerge, scholars and jurists within the Islāmic tradition engage in ongoing discussions and interpretations to address ethical challenges and adapt the principles of Islāmic ethics to contemporary issues. However, no matter the sociocultural variance or differences in scholarly perspectives to emerging issues, at their core, Islāmic ethics honour humans, enjoin them to do good to themselves and one another, validate their freedom of choice, and hold them accountable for their choices (good or bad).

1.2 Islām and Psychology: The Convergence

Considering the role of Islāmic ethics in shaping the psyche and behaviour of Muslims, one begins to understand why religion must be considered in discussions of psychology. The intersection of Islām and psychology is grounded in integrating Islāmic principles and values with psychological theories and practices. This approach acknowledges that religious beliefs and practices substantially influence individuals' mental well-being and behaviour. Positioned within the broader field of psychology, this approach seeks to furnish a comprehensive understanding of human psychology shaped by Islāmic teachings and concepts.

Islāmic psychology recognises the spiritual dimension of human existence, highlighting the pivotal role of faith and spirituality in mental health. Fundamental Islāmic tenets, such as *Tawhîd*, the belief in the accountability of actions in the afterlife (*Yawm al-Qiyâmah*), and the imperative of seeking knowledge and self-improvement (*Talab al-'Ilm*), *Tazkiyat an-Nafs* (purification of the soul or self), Ihsân (perfection or excellence), are incorporated into its framework. Islāmic psychology underscores the interconnection of the mind, body, and soul, championing holistic approaches to well-being. In essence, Islāmic psychology bridges the gap between spirituality and mental health, enriching the understanding of human psychology through the lens of Islāmic philosophy.

This intersection is particularly relevant to our understanding of issues surrounding mental health within Muslim communities. Islāmic psychology acknowledges the cultural and religious context in which individuals live and aims to provide culturally sensitive and relevant psychological interventions. It integrates psychological principles with Islāmic teachings to offer guidance on issues such as anxiety, depression, addiction, and marital conflicts from an Islāmic perspective (Rassool, 2015). At this point, examining Islāmic psychology and what it constitutes is crucial.

1.3 Exploring Islāmic Psychology

Islāmic psychology is a rich and evolving field that seeks to integrate Islāmic principles and values with psychological theories and practices. It recognises the impact of religious beliefs and practices on mental well-being and aims to provide culturally sensitive and relevant psychological interventions within Muslim communities. By incorporating Islāmic teachings and concepts, Islāmic psychology offers a holistic understanding of human psychology. It promotes approaches to well-being that encompass the spiritual, psychological, and social dimensions of individuals' lives. For example, Islāmic psychology addresses mental health concerns from the perspectives of both Islām and psychology. Four key areas are considered below.

One area where the intersection of Islām and psychology has been explored is in the treatment of anxiety disorders. Anxiety is a common mental health issue that affects people of all backgrounds, including Muslims. Islāmic psychology recognises that excessive worry and anxiety can stem from a lack of trust in God's plan or a weak connection to spirituality (Parrott, 2017). While addressing anxiety from the Islāmic perspective, psychologists emphasise the importance of relying on God and developing strong faith as a means of finding comfort and peace. They encourage individuals to engage in prayer, recitation of the Qur'ân, and other acts of worship to alleviate anxiety. Islāmic psychology also promotes the practice of mindfulness and self-reflection, which can help individuals become more aware of their anxious thoughts and develop strategies to manage them.

Another area where the intersection of Islām and psychology is relevant is in the treatment of depression. Depression is a debilitating condition that affects one's ability to function and find joy in life. Islāmic psychology acknowledges that depression can have both psychological and spiritual causes and that a multifaceted approach is required for its treatment (Haque et al., 2016; Haque & Keshavarzi, 2014). One practical answer to managing depression from an Islāmic perspective is to encourage individuals to seek solace in prayers and the remembrance of God. Islāmic psychology also emphasises the importance of seeking social support within the Muslim community and engaging in acts of charity and service to others. This approach is based on the conviction that acts of kindness and service can bring a sense of purpose and fulfilment, which can be particularly beneficial for individuals experiencing depression.

Islāmic psychology equally contributes to the treatment of different forms of addiction, such as substance use disorder and gambling, among others. Addiction has long been identified as a social menace that requires radical solutions. It typically has devastating effects on individuals, families, and communities. Islāmic psychology recognises that addiction is a spiritual and psychological disease and incorporates principles of Islāmic ethics and morality into its treatment. This may include a measure of self-discipline, self-control, and avoiding harmful behaviours. Islāmic psychology also encourages individuals to seek repentance and forgiveness as a means of breaking free from addictive patterns. Additionally, psychologists may work with individuals to develop healthy coping mechanisms and address underlying psychological issues that contribute to addiction.

Islāmic psychology is similarly indispensable in the management of marital conflicts. Marriage is considered a sacred institution in Islām, and it has been proven that conflicts within the family unit have direct or attendant implications on the mental health of all parties involved. Islāmic psychology recognises the importance of maintaining healthy relationships and offers conflict resolution and communication guidance. Psychologists working at the intersection of Islām and psychology may draw on Islāmic concepts of mercy, compassion, and forgiveness to guide couples in resolving conflicts. They may also encourage individuals to seek Islāmic psychotherapy, counselling, and mediation services, which can provide a culturally sensitive and faith-based approach to addressing marital issues.

1.4 Islāmic Ethics and Islāmic Psychology: The Intersection

To understand the ethical foundations of Islāmic psychology, it is imperative to explore the concept of ethics in Islām. As scholars such as Al-Attas (1995) have elucidated, Islāmic ethics is inseparable from the broader worldview of Islām, encompassing the concepts of *Tawhîd* (oneness of God) and *Ma'ārifah* (knowledge of God). On the one hand, the concept of *Tawhîd* lays the groundwork for understanding the unity and interconnectedness of all creation. On the other hand, Ma'ārifah underscores the importance of seeking knowledge to understand and fulfil one's ethical obligations. This pursuit of knowledge is not limited to religious teachings; it extends to various disciplines that contribute to the betterment of society. Ma'ārifah promotes intellectual curiosity and a commitment to lifelong learning.

Several principles of Islāmic ethics are premised on the belief in the supremacy and oneness of God and the adoption of a holistic approach to knowledge. Furthermore, exploring these ethical principles derived from the Qur'ân and the *Sunnah* reveals a comprehensive moral philosophy that guides individual conduct and societal relations. Justice, compassion, and integrity emerge as central virtues in Islāmic ethics, shaping the moral compass of Muslims. Perpetuating these virtues in societal relations requires a strong understanding of *Tawhîd* and the possession of Ma'ārifah.

The Qur'ân, as the primary guidance source, demonstrates these virtues' centrality. It contains numerous verses emphasising justice and fairness in dealings with others, regardless of differences in faith, ethnicity, or social standing. Compassion, derived from the teachings and practices of Prophet Muhammad (ﷺ), extends beyond mere sympathy, urging believers to engage in acts of kindness and charity actively. Integrity, rooted in the consistency between one's beliefs and actions, is highlighted as a cornerstone of ethical behaviour.

In essence, the theological foundations of Islāmic ethics provide a robust and integrated framework that extends beyond individual morality to encompass societal well-being and the harmony of the broader cosmic order. By emphasising the interconnectedness of God, humanity, and the universe and embracing the requisite virtues, Islāmic ethics offers a profound guide for navigating the complexities of human existence and fostering a harmonious and just society. This holistic approach to ethics enriches the individual's spiritual journey and contributes to the collective welfare of communities guided by these principles. This is a fundamental reason Islāmic ethics has continued to find relevance in psychology, providing ethical solutions to mental health problems from the Islāmic perspective.

Islāmic ethics and other related concepts are discussed in Chapter 2, where this book delves into the theological foundations of Islāmic ethics, exploring a pivotal aspect of the framework: the interconnectedness of God, humanity, and the universe. This chapter discusses key ethical principles derived from the Qur'ân and the *Sunnah*, emphasising the centrality of the three virtues highlighted above (justice, compassion, and integrity) in Islāmic moral philosophy. This theological perspective fosters a profound sense of responsibility towards the environment, fellow beings, and oneself, as everything is interconnected and interdependent.

Building upon the conceptual understanding of Islāmic ethics, Chapter 3 explores the process of moral development in the context of Islāmic psychology. Islāmic psychology recognises individuals' innate moral disposition (*fitrah*) and the potential for growth and refinement. Scholars like Al-Ghazālī (1058–1111) have extensively written on the stages of moral development, emphasising the importance of self-awareness, self-discipline, and spiritual purification. Consequently, Chapter 3 examines these stages alongside the psychological dimensions of moral development, drawing insights from classical Islāmic literature and contemporary psychology. This chapter discusses the role of family, community, and spiritual practices in shaping ethical character, providing a comprehensive understanding of how Islāmic psychology views the progression of moral consciousness.

As the field of Islāmic psychology integrates into the broader psychological landscape, practitioners encounter unique ethical dilemmas and challenges. Chapter 4 navigates these complexities, exploring cultural competence, confidentiality, and the integration of Islāmic principles into therapeutic interventions. Drawing from real-world scenarios, this chapter provides insights into navigating the ethical intricacies faced by practitioners working within the framework of Islāmic psychology.

Recognising the need for a systematic approach to ethical conduct in Islāmic psychology, Chapter 5 presents a set of ethical guidelines for Muslim psychologists. These guidelines are rooted in Islāmic principles and address issues of competence, confidentiality, and the incorporation of spirituality into therapeutic practices. This chapter also explores the importance of ongoing professional development and supervision within the context of Islāmic ethical norms.

In the contemporary world, social justice has become a pressing concern. Chapter 6 examines the intersection of Islāmic ethics and social justice, exploring how Islāmic principles guide the pursuit of a just and equitable society. Drawing on Islāmic teachings on economic justice, human rights, and societal harmony, this chapter contributes to the ongoing discourse on Islāmic contributions to social justice. Research ethics in Islāmic psychology is a critical aspect that deserves dedicated attention. Chapter 7 explores the Islāmic ethical considerations in conducting research that involves human participants. It examines principles such as informed consent, beneficence, and respect for autonomy from an Islāmic perspective, contributing to developing ethical standards for research within the field of Islāmic psychology. The concluding chapter synthesises key insights from the preceding chapters, emphasising the importance of advancing ethical considerations within the field of Islāmic psychology. It highlights potential avenues for future research and development, calling for a continued exploration of ethical principles in tandem with the evolving landscape of psychology and Islāmic thought.

In this book, we embark on a journey that explores the theoretical foundations of Islāmic ethics in psychology and provides practical guidance for psychologists and researchers working within the Islāmic framework. As the field continues to evolve, the ethical considerations outlined in this book aim to serve as compasses guiding professionals in their pursuit of the psychological well-being of society, rooted in the profound wisdom of Islāmic ethics.

References

Al-Attas, S. M. N. (1995). Islām: The concept of religion and the foundation of ethics and morality. In *Prolegomena to the metaphysics of Islām: An exposition of the fundamental elements of the worldview of Islām*. International Institute of Islāmic Thought and Civilization (ISTAC).

Askari, H., Iqbal, Z., & Mirakhor, A. (2014). *Introduction to Islāmic economics: Theory and application*. John Wiley & Sons.

Benthall, J. (2003). The greening of Islām? *Anthropology Today*, *19*(6), 10–12.

Chapra, M. U. (2016). *The future of economics: An Islāmic perspective* (Vol. 21). Kube Publishing Ltd.

Davari, M. T. (2004). *The political thought of Ayatollah Murtaza Mutahhari: An Iranian theoretician of the Islāmic state*. Routledge.

El-Rouayheb, K., & Schmidtke, S. (2016). *The Oxford handbook of Islāmic philosophy*. Oxford University Press.

Foltz, R. (2003). *Islām and ecology: A bestowed trust*. Center for the Study of World Religions, Harvard Divinity School.

Haque, A., & Keshavarzi, H. (2014). Integrating indigenous healing methods in therapy: Muslim beliefs and practices. *International Journal of Culture and Mental Health*, *7*(3), 297–314.

Haque, A., Khan, F., Keshavarzi, H., & Rothman, A. E. (2016). Integrating Islāmic traditions in modern psychology: Research trends in last ten years. *Journal of Muslim Mental Health*, *10*(1).

Khan, M. A. (1992). *Theoretical studies in Islāmic banking and finance*. Theoretical Studies in Islāmic Banking and Finance.
Mahallati, M. J. A. (2016). *Ethics of war and peace in Iran and Shi'i Islām*. University of Toronto Press.
Nuriz, M. A. F., & Awang, J. (n.d.). Religious pluralism: The influence of rationalism and relativism on Muslim scholars. *International Advisory Board, 31*.
Parrott, J. (2017). *How to be a mindful Muslim: An exercise in Islāmic meditation*. Irving, TX: Yaqeen Institute for Islamic Research, 2017. https://yaqeeninstitute.org/read/paper/how-to-be-a-mindful-muslim
Pusch, B. (2016). The greening of Islāmic politics: A godsend for the environment? In *Environmentalism in Turkey* (pp. 145–160). Routledge.
Rassool, G. H. (2015). *Islāmic counselling: An introduction to theory and practice*. Routledge.
Tibi, B. (2017). War and peace in Islām. In *The Use of Force in International Law* (pp. 47–64). Routledge.
Zuhaili, W. (1985) 'Al Fiqh al Islami Wa Adillatuhu (Vol. 8)', Damaskus: Dar al Fikr. s [Preprint].

Part I

Foundations of Islāmic Ethics

2 The Concept of Ethics in Islām

2.1 Introduction

Ethics plays a crucial role in shaping the moral framework of any religious and cultural system. As explained in Chapter 1, ethics in Islām is deeply rooted in the teachings of the Qur'ân, the sayings and actions of the Prophet Muhammad, known as *Hādīth* and *Sunnah*, and the principles derived from these sources. Islāmic ethics provide comprehensive guidelines for Muslims in their personal and social conduct, encompassing various aspects of life, including spirituality, morality, justice and compassion. This chapter explores the concept of ethics in Islām, examining the Qur'ânic perspective, the role of *Hādīths*, and the principles that form the foundation of Islāmic ethics. (Hashi, 2011)

2.2 Interrogating Islāmic Ethics Based on Qur'ânic Precepts

One of the key references to the Qur'ân as the primary source of Islāmic ethics, *Surah Al-Nahl* (The Bee) Qur'ân (16:90), has been presented in Chapter 1. In this verse, Allāh says:

إن الله يأمركم بالعدل والإحسان وإيتاء ذي القربى وينهى عن الفحشاء والمنكر
والبغي يعظكم لعلكم تذكرون

Indeed, Allāh orders justice and good conduct and giving to relatives and forbids immorality and bad conduct and oppression. He admonishes you that perhaps you will be reminded.

This verse is evidence that the Qur'ân presents a moral framework encompassing every aspect of human life, including a wide range of ethical teachings, principles, and values. It serves as a critical source of guidance for Muslims; the Qur'ân provides guidelines for personal conduct, social interactions, business transactions, governance, and more. It lays down clear Muslim guidelines, serving as a divine roadmap for leading a virtuous and ethical life (Esposito, 2004).

DOI: 10.4324/9781032658858-3

The Qur'ân also stresses the importance of righteousness, justice, honesty, and compassion, among other virtues. Verses depicting the pertinence of each of these virtues are presented below. Further discussions on the concepts of righteousness, justice, and honesty are presented in Section 2.3, the section on Islāmic ethical principles.

- **Righteousness**: Emphasising the need for righteousness (*Taqwa*), Allāh says in the Qur'ân (59:18):

  يأيها الذين ءامنوا اتقوا الله ولتنظر نفس ما قدمت لغد

  O you who have believed, fear Allāh. And let every soul look to what it has put forth for tomorrow.

- **Justice**: In the Qur'ân (4:135), Allāh commands Muslims to maintain justice, even at the detriment of personal or familial gain. Allāh says:

  يأيها الذين ءامنوا كونوا قوامين بالقسط شهدآء لله ولو على أنفسكم أو الوالدين والأقربين

  O you who have believed, be persistently standing firm in justice, witnesses for Allāh, even if it be against yourselves or parents and relative.

- **Honesty**: The Qur'ân (2:188) highlights the need for honesty in all one's dealings:

  ولا تأكلوا أموالكم بينكم بالباطل وتدلوا بها إلى الحكّام لتأكلوا فريقا من أموال الناس بالإثم وأنتم تعلمون

  And do not consume one another's wealth unjustly or send it [in bribery] to the rulers in order that [they might aid] you [to] consume a portion of the wealth of the people in sin, while you know [it is unlawful].

- **Compassion**: Two exceedingly relevant verses on exercising compassion and mercy are provided here. Qur'ân (42:39–40) states:

  والذين إذا أصابهم البغي هم ينتصرون. وجزآء سيئة سيئة مثلها فمن عفا وأصلح فأجره على الله

  "And those who, when tyranny strikes them, they defend themselves. And the retribution for an evil act is an evil one like it, but whoever pardons and makes reconciliation – his reward is [due] from Allāh". Qur'ân (25:63) passes a similar message:

  وعباد الرحمان الذين يمشون على الأرض هونا وإذا خاطبهم الجاهلون قالوا سلما

  And the servants of the Most Merciful are those who walk upon the earth easily, and when the ignorant address them [harshly], they say [words of] peace.

- **General Guidance**: In multiple verses, Allāh explains that the Qur'ân is an unimpeachable source of guidance for mankind. For instance, Qur'ân (2:2) stresses:

ذلك الكتاب لا ريب فيه هدى للمتقين

"This is the Book about which there is no doubt, a guidance for those conscious of Allāh", and Qur'ân (15:87) adds;

ولقد ءاتيناك سبعا من المثاني والقرءان العظيم

"And We have certainly given you, [O Muhammad], seven of the often repeated [verses] and the great Qur'ân".

- **Good Intention**: The Qur'ân also stresses the need to back ethical actions with good intention. Muslims are encouraged to perform good deeds with sincere and pure intentions, seeking only the pleasure of God and not solely to pursue worldly recognition or personal gain. This focus on intention underscores the internal dimension of ethics, highlighting the significance of one's inner state and motivation in determining the ethical value of an action.

In emphasising the importance of aligning ethical actions with virtuous intentions, the Qur'ân delves into the profound connection between outward behaviour and inner sincerity. The Islāmic teachings underscore that the merit of a deed lies not only in the observable act itself; rather, it is profoundly intertwined with the purity of the intention behind it. This emphasis cultivates a deep sense of mindfulness and self-awareness, urging individuals to introspect and ensure that their actions are guided by a genuine desire to please God rather than by external factors such as public recognition or personal benefit.

In doing so, the Qur'ân guides believers to forge a moral compass that transcends life's superficial and materialistic aspects, fostering a profound sense of spirituality and moral responsibility. This emphasis on the internal dimension of ethics resonates with the broader Islāmic worldview, wherein aligning actions and intentions is pivotal in establishing a harmonious and righteous society. To further highlight its significance in Islāmic ethics, verses emphasise the need for good intention and the connection between outward actions and inner sincerity. These include Al-Baqarah (2:197), Al-Mulk (67:2), and Al-Hashr (59:18–19), among others.

- **Brotherhood:** The Qur'ânic concept of brotherhood promotes solidarity among Muslims. Allāh says in Surah Al-Imran (Qur'ân, 3:103):

واعتصموا بحبل الله جميعا ولا تفرقوا واذكروا نعمت الله عليكم إذ كنتم أعداء فألف بين قلوبكم فأصبحتم بنعمته إخوانا وكنتم على شفا حفرة من النار فأنقذكم منها. . .

> And hold firmly to the rope of Allāh all together and do not become divided. And remember the favour of Allāh upon you – when you were enemies and He brought your hearts together and you became, by His favour, brothers. And you were on the edge of a pit of the fire.

Beyond brotherhood among Muslims, the Qur'ân encourages Muslims to work towards improving society. This concept extends beyond the boundaries of the Muslim community, as the Qur'ân recognises the inherent value and worth of all human beings. Muslims are called upon to be compassionate and merciful towards others, especially those who are vulnerable or in need. Acts of charity, kindness, and generosity are highly regarded in Islām and are considered integral aspects of ethical behaviour (Afsaruddin, 2017).

- **Intra and Interpersonal Relationships**: The Qur'ân also emphasises the importance of the individual's relationship with self. It encourages self-reflection, self-discipline, and self-improvement. Muslims are urged to develop humility, patience, gratitude, and perseverance. They are encouraged to strive for excellence in all aspects of life, seeking knowledge, and engaging in continuous self-improvement. Muslims are also encouraged to treat others with kindness, justice, and respect. The Qur'ân promotes the values of honesty, integrity, and trustworthiness in business dealings, emphasising the prohibition of dishonest practices such as usury and exploitation. Muslims are urged to be mindful of their words and actions; to avoid backbiting, slander, and gossip; and to promote unity, cooperation, and harmony within their communities.

The Qur'ânic perspective on ethics also addresses the ethical implications of various contemporary issues. While the Qur'ân was revealed over 1,400 years ago, its principles are considered timeless and applicable to the present day. Muslims are encouraged to interpret and apply the Qur'ânic teachings in a way that addresses the ethical challenges of their time while remaining grounded in the fundamental principles of the faith. For example, the Qur'ân mentions the importance of environmental stewardship and protecting the Earth's resources. Muslims are called "responsible custodians" of the environment, avoiding wastefulness and excessive consumption and taking measures to preserve and sustain the natural world. These can be achieved by promoting sustainable practices, conserving water, and respecting the rights of animals (Al-Attar, 2010).

These references showcase the Qur'ân's emphasis on moral values, ethical conduct, and guidance for various aspects of human life, including personal behaviour, social justice, and interpersonal relations. They underscore the importance of righteousness, justice, honesty, and compassion in the life of a believer. Islāmic ethics, rooted in the principles outlined above, permeate all aspects of Muslim life. These principles are not meant to be abstract concepts but are intended to be embodied in daily actions and interactions. Through the application of these principles, Muslims seek to achieve personal growth, maintain strong moral character, and contribute to the betterment of society (Omar, 2013).

2.3 Representations of Islāmic Ethics in the *Hādīth* and Prophetic Teachings

In addition to the Qur'ân, the *Hādīth* and *Sunnah*, the sayings and actions of the Prophet Muhammad (ﷺ) provide further guidance on ethical conduct. They contain practical examples of how the Prophet lived out the teachings of the Qur'ân in his daily life. They serve as sources of guidance for Muslims, offering insights into the Prophet's character, interactions with others, and ethical conduct. This is because Prophet Muhammad (ﷺ) is considered the epitome of moral excellence and serves as a role model for Muslims. His teachings and actions exemplify the ethical ideals that Muslims strive to emulate daily and are significant in shaping Islāmic ethics.

For the role of the *hādīth* in shaping Islāmic ethics, you can refer to a well-known *hādīth* from Sahih al-Bukhari, one of the most respected collections of *Hādīth*. In this *hādīth*, "The Prophet Muhammad (ﷺ) said: 'I have been sent to perfect the good character'". The *hādīth* emphasises the importance of good character and ethical conduct, a central theme in Islāmic ethics. Islāmic ethics is primarily embodied in numerous collections of *hādīths*, and the importance of *hādīth* in shaping various ethical values cannot be overstated. *Hādīth* serves as a practical guide for Muslims, offering specific examples and scenarios that illustrate how to embody the ethical principles outlined in the Qur'ân. Muslims look to the *hādīth* for specific guidance on various issues, including personal hygiene, family relations, personal ethics, social interactions, marriage, charity, business dealings, and governance.

Muslim scholars have meticulously studied, classified, and authenticated *hādīth* narrations to ensure their reliability and authenticity. Authenticated *hādīth* have been compiled into a body of *hādīth* literature, including collections such as *Ṣahih Bukhârî* and *Ṣahih Muslim*. *Hādīth* literature is a valuable source for Muslims to understand the Prophet's ethical teachings and apply them in their lives. It offers detailed insights into the Prophet's character and interactions with others and emphasises virtuous character. *Hādīth* literature complements the Qur'ân and helps to contextualise and further elucidate its ethical teachings (Al-Fadli, 2011). Through studying and reflecting upon the *hādīth* and Prophetic traditions, Muslims gain a deeper understanding of the Qur'ânic teachings and how to implement them in various aspects of life.

For a comprehensive reference on the significance of *hādīth* in Islāmic ethics and its role in shaping ethical values, the work *Usool-Al-Hadeeth: The Methodology of Hādīth Evaluation* Philips (2007) can be considered. The book provides an in-depth exploration of the science of *hādīth*, its authenticity, and its application in understanding and practising Islāmic ethics. It also offers valuable insights into the relationship between the Qur'ân and *hādīth*, emphasising the practical guidance that *hādīth* provides for Muslims in applying ethical principles in their daily lives (Philips, 2007).

Generally, *hādīth* literature, in explaining and providing practical applications of Qur'ânic injunctions, tends to emphasise *Akhlaq*, or morality. This encompasses a wide range of virtues that Muslims are encouraged to embody. These are honesty, integrity, humility, patience, gratitude, and forgiveness. These virtues are not limited to specific contexts but are meant to be practised in all aspects of life, guiding Muslims in their relationships, professional endeavours, and personal growth (Al-Nawawi, 1855). Some prophetic perspectives on ethics and virtues are considered below to better contextualise this.

- **Governance and Leadership**: There are many examples in *hādīth* literature concerning the Prophetic traditions on governance and leadership. The Prophet Muhammad's (ﷺ) example as a just and compassionate leader is considered a model for Muslim rulers and administrators. His *hādīth* narrations guide issues such as consultation, justice, accountability, and the equitable distribution of resources. They highlight the importance of good governance and the ethical responsibilities of those in positions of authority (Azami, 2002).
- **Humility**: Humility is another virtue that is emphasised in Prophetic ethics. The Prophet Muhammad (ﷺ) was known for his humility and modesty despite his elevated status as a leader and a messenger of God. His humility is evident in his interactions with people from all walks of life and his refusal to be treated as superior. *Hādīth* narrations capture his humble demeanour and guide cultivating humility in one's character. For instance, the Prophet (ﷺ) said, "He who humbles himself for the sake of Allāh, Allāh raises him in rank". This *hādīth* encourages Muslims to embrace humility as a means of drawing closer to Allāh and seeking His favour (Ramadan, 2006).
- **Compassion and Kindness**: Another significant aspect of Prophetic ethics found in *hādīth* is the emphasis on compassion and kindness towards others, young and old. The Prophet Muhammad (ﷺ) was known for his compassion and empathy towards everyone, regardless of social status, age, or religious affiliation. His *hādīth* narrations reflect this compassionate spirit and encourage Muslims to follow in his footsteps. For example, he said, "He who is not kind to people, Allāh is not kind to him". This *hādīth* teaches Muslims the importance of treating others with kindness and compassion, fostering a sense of empathy and goodwill within society (Alharbi & Al Hadid, 2019).
- **Forgiveness**: Forgiveness is yet another ethical value deeply rooted in the teachings of the Prophet Muhammad (ﷺ). He consistently demonstrated

forgiveness, even in the face of personal harm. *Hādīth* narrations recount instances where the Prophet forgave those wronged him and advised his followers to do the same. One well-known *hādīth* states, "The best among you are those who are best in character and who forgive when they are wronged". This *hādīth* highlights the virtue of forgiveness and encourages Muslims to let go of grudges, promote reconciliation, and maintain harmonious relationships with others.

Overall, the references discussed above highlight the Qur'ân and *hādīth* as the foundational sources of Islāmic ethics and can support the idea that Islāmic ethical principles are deeply rooted in and derived from these sources.

2.4 Islāmic Ethical Principles in the Qur'ân and *Hādīth*

From the Qur'ân and *hādīth*, certain principles emerge that form the foundation of Islāmic ethics. A foundational concept to consider is *Maqasid al-Shar'iah,* which refers to the higher objectives and purposes of Islāmic law (Auda, 2022). It provides a framework for understanding the goals and intentions behind specific Islāmic rulings, emphasising preserving faith, life, dignity, lineage, and property. This principle helps Muslims navigate ethical dilemmas by considering the broader objectives of Islāmic law and the welfare of individuals and society (Ashur, 2006; Kamali, 1999; Murata & Chittick, 2006). Based on this, five principles of Islāmic ethics are considered below.

2.5 Principle 1: *Tawhîd*

One of the fundamental ethical principles in Islām is the concept of *Tawhîd*, the belief in the oneness of God. This belief forms the basis of all ethical considerations in Islām, as it acknowledges God's authority and the accountability of human beings to their Creator. Muslims are expected to reflect this belief, recognising that their actions have consequences in this world and the hereafter. *Tawhîd* instils in Muslims a profound sense of purpose and responsibility that permeates every aspect of their lives. It is a fundamental tenet of the Islāmic faith that serves as the cornerstone of a Muslim's worldview, shaping their understanding of themselves, their relationships with others, and their role in the world (Philips, 2006).

At its core, *Tawhîd* emphasises the absolute unity and uniqueness of God. Muslims believe in a monotheistic deity who is the Creator and Sustainer of the universe, transcending all human comprehension. This belief instils in them a deep reverence for God and a recognition of His absolute authority over all aspects of existence. It serves as a constant reminder that their actions are ultimately accountable to Him, and they must strive to align their behaviour with His teachings (Philips, 1994). The belief in *Tawhîd* acts as a guiding light, illuminating the path of righteousness for Muslims. It reminds them that their purpose is to worship and serve God, seek His pleasure, and follow His commandments.

This recognition of divine purpose infuses their actions with a higher meaning and encourages them to live with integrity, sincerity, and righteousness, regardless of their circumstances (Al-Faruqi, 1992). When humans understand that their actions are accountable to God, it fosters a deep sense of moral responsibility. They realise their choices and behaviour have consequences in this life and the hereafter. This awareness prompts them to reflect on their actions' ethical implications and strive for excellence in all their endeavours.

Tawhîd also accentuates the importance of sincerity in worship and daily interactions. Muslims are encouraged to perform acts of worship, such as prayer, fasting, and charity, with pure and sincere intention, solely to please God. This emphasis on sincerity extends beyond acts of worship to encompass all aspects of life, encouraging Muslims to be sincere in their relationships, work, and dealings with others. Furthermore, the belief in *Tawhîd* fosters a sense of humility and gratitude in Muslims. They acknowledge that everything they have, in material possessions, talents, and opportunities, is ultimately a gift from God. This understanding cultivates a mindset of gratitude and contentment, enabling Muslims to appreciate the blessings in their lives (Philips, 1994).

Another dimension to the concept of *Tawhîd* in Islāmic ethics is its profound implications for social and environmental responsibility. Muslims are reminded that humanity is interconnected, as we are all creations of the same divine being. Moreover, *Tawhîd* calls upon Muslims to be responsible stewards of the Earth. They are entrusted with preserving and protecting the environment as a manifestation of God's creation. This belief motivates them to adopt sustainable practices, conserve resources, and care for the natural world, recognising that they are accountable for their actions towards the planet and future generations (Foltz, 2003).

In general, the belief in *Tawhîd* has a transformative impact on the lives of Muslims. It instils in them a sense of purpose, responsibility, and accountability to God. This belief is a constant reminder to act with integrity, sincerity, and righteousness, shaping their relationships, ethical choices, and engagement with the world. *Tawhîd* empowers Muslims to live purposeful lives dedicated to worship, service, and compassion, striving to create a more just and harmonious society guided by the principles of their faith (Philips, 1989).

2.6 Principle 2: *Taqwa*

Taqwa (which means God-consciousness) is another foundational concept in Islām. Muslims are encouraged to aspire to heightened awareness of God's presence. *Taqwa* is a guiding principle that shapes Muslims' thoughts, actions, and behaviours. With *Taqwa*, individuals are motivated to make ethical decisions guided by the desire to please God and seek His reward (Akrami et al., 2011). Muslims are called upon to cultivate a deep sense of God-consciousness, which involves being mindful of God's presence and seeking to act by His commandments. This awareness of God's presence is a guiding principle in ethical decision-making, promoting a sense of moral responsibility and accountability (Al-Attar, 2010).

At the core of *Taqwa* is the recognition that God is constantly observing and aware of everything, even the most hidden intentions and thoughts. This awareness instils a deep sense of responsibility in Muslims, urging them to lead a righteous and virtuous life. It acts as a moral compass, helping individuals differentiate between right and wrong and navigate the complexities of everyday life (Ohlander, 2005). One of the ways *Taqwa* manifests itself is through self-restraint. One who possesses *Taqwa* exercises caution and self-discipline in their actions and words. One is mindful of the consequences of one's behaviour, not only in the worldly sense but also in one's spiritual journey. This mindfulness encourages one to refrain from actions that may lead astray, such as lying, cheating, or engaging in unethical practices. Instead, one strives to embody honesty, integrity, and compassion in all aspects of one's life.

In the Qur'ân, a relevant reference is Surah Al-Baqarah (2:197), which states:

. . .وتزودوا فإن خير الزاد التقوى واتقون يا أولي الألباب

And take provisions, but indeed, the best provision is fear of Allāh. And fear Me, O you who of understanding.

In this verse, Allāh defines what *Taqwa* is. He clarifies that contrary to the popular misconception that *Taqwa* means total abstinence from worldly provisions, a person's accurate indication of God-consciousness is their ability to fear and obey Allāh in all aspects of their worldly affairs. *Taqwa* also serves as a source of strength and resilience in challenging times. Muslims who possess *Taqwa* find solace and comfort in their unwavering trust in God. They understand that trials and tribulations are a part of life and face them with patience and perseverance. *Taqwa* instils the belief that God is always with them, guiding and protecting them through every problematic encounter (Ranieri, 2022).

Taqwa also promotes a sense of humility and gratitude. Recognising God's infinite power and wisdom, individuals with Taqwa understand their limitations and seek to cultivate a deep sense of humility before their Creator. They acknowledge that everything they have is a blessing from God and, therefore, approach life with gratitude. This gratitude manifests in various ways, such as performing acts of charity, helping those in need, and treating others with kindness and respect. Furthermore, *Taqwa* encourages Muslims to be mindful of their intentions. It emphasises the importance of sincerity in worship and all actions undertaken for the sake of God. Muslims must examine their motives and ensure their actions are not driven by ego, pride, or worldly gains. Instead, they strive to purify their intentions, seeking solely the pleasure and acceptance of God.

2.7 Principle 3: *Ihsân*

Another important principle is the concept of *Ihsân*, which can be translated as "excellence" or "perfection". *Ihsân*, the pursuit of excellence, is a fundamental concept in Islām that goes beyond the minimum requirements of ethical behaviour. It comprises a holistic approach to life, encompassing the development of noble character traits and cultivating virtuous qualities. *Ihsân* requires Muslims to go beyond fulfilling their essential obligations and strive for higher moral and spiritual excellence. It involves worshipping God as if one sees Him, knowing He sees all, even if one cannot see Him. This principle instils accountability and mindfulness in every action, fostering a deeper connection with God and a heightened awareness of ethical responsibilities.

Muslims who strive for *Ihsân* aim to be the best version of themselves, constantly seeking improvement in their conduct and actions. In *The Heart of Islām: Enduring Values for Humanity*, Seyyed Hossein Nasr addresses the spiritual and ethical dimensions of Islām, providing a comprehensive exploration of various aspects of Islām, including the concept of *Ihsân*. The work is a relevant source for understanding the pursuit of excellence in the Islāmic context (Nasr, 2009). In the Islāmic tradition, *Ihsân* is often understood as the highest level of faith, surpassing mere adherence to religious rituals and obligations. It is considered the pinnacle of spirituality, where one's inner state aligns with one's outward actions.

The Prophet Muhammad (ﷺ) described *Ihsân* as "worshipping Allāh as if you see Him, and if you cannot see Him, then know that He sees you". This encapsulates the essence of *Ihsân*, which involves recognising the presence of the Divine in all aspects of life and conducting oneself accordingly (Al-Ghazālī, 2007). Muslims are encouraged to cultivate virtuous qualities and character traits to embody Ihsân. These include sincerity (*Ikhlas*), patience (*sabr*), gratitude (*shukr*), humility (*tawadu'*), forgiveness (*'afu*), and compassion (*rahma*), among others. By internalising these qualities, Muslims strive to attain excellence in their relationships with Allāh, themselves, and others (Al-Haddad, 2003).

In pursuing *Ihsân*, Muslims understand that excellence is not a destination but a journey of continuous self-improvement. It requires introspection, self-discipline, and a willingness to acknowledge one's shortcomings. Muslims are encouraged to self-reflect, regularly assess their thoughts, intentions, and actions, and seek areas for growth and improvement. *Ihsân* is not an easy path; it requires continuous effort, self-discipline, and resilience. However, Muslims believe that the rewards of *Ihsân* are immense, both in this world and the hereafter. By embodying *Ihsân*, Muslims strive to attain a state of spiritual fulfilment, inner peace, and closeness to Allāh.

Moreover, *Ihsân* extends beyond individual behaviour to encompass societal and communal responsibilities. Muslims are called to contribute positively to their communities, seeking justice, fairness, and equality. This includes acts of charity, volunteering, advocating for social justice, and promoting the well-being of others. By actively engaging in acts of kindness and service, Muslims aim to impact the world around them positively. Through the pursuit of excellence, Muslims aspire to fulfil their purpose in life, seeking to make a positive difference in the world while continuously striving to improve themselves (Syafi'i, n.d.).

2.8 Principle 4: *'Adl*

Islāmic ethics also strongly emphasises the principle of *'Adl* (justice). The Qur'ân repeatedly emphasises the importance of upholding justice, treating others fairly, and standing up against oppression and injustice. Verses 8 and 7–9 in Surah Al-Mai'dah and Ar-Rahman are principal examples. In Surah Al-Mai'dah (Qur'ân, 5:8), Allāh directly instructs Muslims to be just as a way of showing God-consciousness;

يــأيها الذين ءامنوا كونوا قوامين لله شهداء بالقسط.

O you who have believed, be persistently standing firm for Allāh, witnesses in justice.

In Surah Ar-Rahman (Qur'ân, 55:7–9), Allāh describes justice as requisite for maintaining societal balance;

والسماء رفعها ووضعها الميزان. ألا تطغوا في الميزان. وأقيموا الوزن بالقسط ولا تخسروا الميزان

And the heaven He raised and imposed the balance. That you not transgress within the balance. And establish weight in justice and do not make deficient the balance.

Justice is a fundamental concept in Islāmic ethics and an integral part of the Islāmic faith. It permeates every Muslim's life, shaping their relationships with others and guiding their actions. The concept of justice in Islām goes beyond mere legality; it encompasses a moral obligation to treat all individuals fairly and with compassion (Zaroug, 1999). In Qur'ân (4:58) Allāh says:

إن الله يأمركم أن تؤدوا الأمانات إلى أهلها وإذا حكمت بين الناس أن تحكموا بالعدل إن الله نعما يعظكم به إن الله كان سميعا بصيرا

"Indeed, Allāh commands you to render trusts to whom they are due and when you judge between people to judge with justice. Excellent is that which Allāh instructs you. Indeed, Allāh is ever Hearing and Seeing". This verse calls for fairness, compassion and equality in all dealings with everyone.

The verses presented depict the place of *'Adl* as a cornerstone in Islāmic ethics and a guiding principle for Muslims in all aspects of life. One of the key foundations of Islāmic justice is the concept of equality. Muslims believe that all human beings are equal in the eyes of Allāh, regardless of race, ethnicity, social status, or gender. The Qur'ân explicitly states:

يأيها الناس إنا خلقناكم من ذكر وأنثى وجعلناكم شعوبا وقبائل لتعارفوا إن
أكرمكم عند الله أتقاكم إن الله عليم خبير

O mankind, indeed We have created you from male and female and made you peoples and tribes that you may know one another. Indeed, the most noble of you in the sight of Allāh is the most righteous of you. Indeed, Allāh is Knowing and Acquainted.

(Qur'ân 49:13)

This verse emphasises the importance of righteousness and piety rather than superficial factors in determining one's worth. Muslims are encouraged to promote social justice, fight against discrimination, and work towards the eradication of poverty and inequality. By upholding the principles of justice and compassion, Muslims strive to create a world free from injustice and inequality, where all people can live with dignity and harmony.

In promoting equity and equality, Islāmic ethics champions a just society where the rights of all individuals are protected and respected, and oppression is actively fought against. To this end, Islāmic law or *Shari'ah* is crucial in promoting justice in Muslim societies. *Shari'ah* encompasses legal matters and moral and ethical principles that guide personal conduct. It is intended to protect the rights of individuals and uphold justice, ensuring that the vulnerable and marginalised members of society are safeguarded and their rights respected (Dhar, 2013).

Islāmic social justice extends beyond individual interactions to encompass broader societal issues. For instance, *zakāt*, one of the five pillars of Islām, is a form of obligatory charity to alleviate poverty and provide for people in need. Muslims must give a portion of their wealth to support the less fortunate and ensure the equitable distribution of resources within the community. This practice fosters a sense of responsibility and solidarity, reinforcing the principles of justice and compassion. Moreover, aside from fostering justice between humans, the principle of justice in Islam also extends to treating animals and the environment. Animals and nature are believed to be trusts handed over to humanity for safekeeping. Consequently, Islām promotes the responsible stewardship of resources and the prohibition of unnecessary harm.

Islām also emphasises the principle of retribution or *Qisas* to maintain justice. *Qisas* is the principle of equal retaliation for a crime committed, ensuring that the punishment matches the severity of the offence. However, forgiveness is highly encouraged in Islām, and there are opportunities for the victim or their family to pardon the offender, promoting reconciliation and fostering a spirit of mercy and compassion. Furthermore, Islāmic ethics demand that Muslims avoid any form of discrimination or oppression. The Prophet Muhammad (ﷺ) set a powerful example in his treatment of others, regardless of their faith or background. He championed the rights of minorities, advocated for women's rights and emphasised the fair treatment of enslaved people. His just and compassionate actions remain a guiding light for Muslims striving to follow his teachings today (Khadduri, 1966; Ramadan, 2006).

In times of conflict and war, Islām provides clear guidelines on just conduct, including the protection of civilians, prisoners of war, and the environment. The concept of *Jihad*, often misunderstood, refers to a struggle against oppression and injustice, whether on a personal, social or political level. *Jihad* does not condone violence against innocent civilians or unprovoked aggression but emphasises the necessity of standing up against oppression. Throughout history, there have been remarkable examples of Muslim scholars, leaders, and individuals who have championed justice and fought against oppression. Their faith has motivated them to speak out against tyranny and work tirelessly to establish societies based on justice and compassion (Hashmi, 1996).

2.9 Principle 5: Honesty

Muslims are encouraged to speak the truth, even under challenging circumstances, and to uphold their promises and covenants. The prohibition of lying, cheating, and engaging in deceptive practices is emphasised, as these actions undermine trust and integrity in relationships and society. One of the key ethical principles emphasised in the *hādīth* is honesty. The Prophet Muhammad (ﷺ) emphasised truthfulness and integrity in personal and business dealings. He was known for his impeccable honesty and earned the title *Al-Amin*, meaning "the trustworthy". His sayings and actions regarding honesty have been recorded in numerous *hādīth* narrations. For instance, he stated, "Truthfulness leads to righteousness, and righteousness leads to Paradise". This *hādīth* underscores the significance of truthfulness and highlights the ultimate reward for those who adhere to it (Kamali, 2022).

References

Afsaruddin, A. (2017). Dying in the path of God: Reading martyrdom and moral excellence in the Qur'ân. In *Roads to Paradise: Eschatology and concepts of the hereafter in Islam (2 vols.)* (pp. 162–180). Brill.

Akrami, S. A., Madigan, D. A., Davis, E. F., Bakar, O., Langan, J. P., Afsaruddin, A., Haleem, M. A., Sanneh, L., Azumah, J., & Saeed, A. (2011).

Communicating the word: Revelation, translation, and interpretation in Christianity and Islam. Georgetown University Press.

Al-Attar, M. (2010). *Islāmic ethics: Divine command theory in Arabo-Islāmic thought*. Routledge.

Al-Fadli, A. al-H. (2011). *Introduction to hādīth*. ICAS Press.

Al-Faruqi, I. R. (1992). *Al Tawhîd: Its implications on thought and life* (Vol. 4). International Institute of Islāmic Thought (IIIT).

Al-Ghazālī, A. H. M. (2007). *Ihya Ulum al-Din: The revival of religious sciences* (F. Karim, Trans., Vol. 4). Kazi Publications.

Al-Haddad, I. A. I. (2003). *The Book of Assistance*. (M. Badawi, Trans.). Fons Vitae.

Al-Nawawī, A. Z. Y. ibn S. (2023). *Riyāḍ al-ṣāliḥīn*. Damascus: Dār al-Faiḥā'.

Alharbi, J., & Al Hadid, L. (2019). Towards an understanding of compassion from an Islāmic perspective. *Journal of Clinical Nursing*, *28*(7–8), 1354–1358.

Ashur, M. A.-T. I. (2006). *Ibn Ashur: Treatise on Maqasid Al-Shariah*. International Institute of Islāmic Thought (IIIT).

Auda, J. (2022). *Maqasid al-Shari'ah as philosophy of Islāmic law*. International Institute of Islāmic Thought (IIIT).

Azami, M. M. (2002). *Studies in hādīth methodology and literature*. The Other Press.

Bilal Philips, A. A. (2007). *Usool-Al-Hadeeth: The methodology of hādīth evaluation*. Riyadh International Islāmic Publishing House.

Dhar, P. (2013). Zakat as a measure of social justice in Islāmic finance: An accountant ' s overview. *Journal of Emerging Economies and Islāmic Research*, *1*(1), 11.

Esposito, J. L. (2004). *The oxford dictionary of Islam*. Oxford University Press.

Foltz, R. (2003). *Islam and ecology: A bestowed trust*. Center for the Study of World Religions, Harvard Divinity School.

Hashi, A. A. (2011). Islāmic ethics: An outline of its principles and scope. *Revelation and Science*, *01*(03), 122–130.

Hashmi, S. H. (1996). Interpreting the Islāmic ethics of war and peace. In *The ethics of war and peace*. Princeton University Press. https://doi.org/10.1515/9780691221854–011

Kamali, M. H. (1999). " Maqāṣid al-Sharī'ah": The Objectives of Islāmic law. *Islāmic Studies*, *38*(2), 193–208.

Kamali, M. H. (2022). Between separation and unity: The interplay of law and morality in Islāmic jurisprudence. *Sharia Law In The Twenty-First Century*, *21*.

Khadduri, M. (1966). *The Islāmic law of nations: Shaybani's Siyar*. JHU Press.

Murata, S., & Chittick, W. C. (2006). *The vision of Islam*. I.B. Tauris. https://books.google.com.ng/books?id=GZJ1O9Xe68EC

Nasr, S. H. (2009). *The heart of Islam: Enduring values for humanity*. Zondervan.

Ohlander, E. S. (2005). Fear of God (Taqwā) in the Qur'ān: Some notes on Semantic shift and thematic context. *Journal of Semitic Studies*, *50*(1), 137–152.

Omar, M. N. (2013). Ethics in Islam: A brief survey. *The Social Sciences*, *8*(5), 387–392.

Philips, A. A. B. (1989). *The fundamentals of Tawheed (Islāmic Monotheism)*. Millat Book Centre. https://books.google.com.my/books?id=8BxlVBPmGlcC

Philips, A. A. B. (1994). *The fundamentals of tawheed (Islāmic Monotheism)*. Islāmic Books.

Philips, A. A. B. (2006). *The evolution of fiqh (Islāmic law & the Madh-habs)*. IslamKotob.

Ramadan, T. (2006). *In the footsteps of the Prophet: Lessons from the life of Muhammad*. Oxford University Press. https://books.google.com.my/books?id=wW2x_iaqKZgC

Ranieri, J. J. (2022). Defending victims, practicing restraint: God-consciousness and the use of force in the Qur'ân. *Religions*, *13*(2), 124.

Syafi'i, A.-I. al-H. (n.d.). Abdullah bin 'Alawi al-Haddad al-Hadrami al. In *Risalat Al-Mu'awana*. Dar Al-Kotob Al-Ilmiyah, 2015.

Zaroug, A. H. (1999). Ethics from an Islāmic perspective: Basic issues. *American Journal of Islam and Society*, *16*(3), 45–63.

3 What Is the Relationship Between Moral Development and Islāmic Ethics?

3.0 Introduction

Moral development is a multifaceted journey that shapes the ethical fabric of an individual, influencing their decisions, actions, and relationships. In the realm of Islāmic psychology, moral development is deeply intertwined with the concept of *fitrah*, the innate disposition that forms the foundational basis of human nature. Islāmic psychology offers a unique perspective on moral growth, emphasising the alignment of one's behaviour with the inherent predisposition towards goodness and virtue. The significance of *fitrah* in moral development lies in its role as an innate compass, guiding individuals towards righteousness. In this chapter, we explore the profound connection between *fitrah* and moral development, unravelling the stages of moral development outlined in Islāmic psychology and delving into the importance of nurturing virtuous character within the Islāmic tradition.

3.1 The Role of *Fitrah* (Innate Disposition) in Moral Development

The concept of *fitrah* holds significant importance in Islāmic theology and psychology, particularly in moral development and character-building. *Fitrah* refers to the innate disposition with which every human being is created. It represents the primordial nature that every human being is born with. It is often described as an inclination towards recognising and embracing moral values instilled in each individual by the Creator. It is believed that Allāh (God) has bestowed upon each individual a pure nature that inclines towards righteousness and moral goodness. The Qur'ân mentions this concept in several verses, emphasising humans' inclination to recognise and adhere to the truth. Allah says:

فأقم وجهك للدين حنيفا فطرت الله التي فطر الناس عليها لا تبديل لخلق الله
ذلك الدين القيم ولكن أكثر الناس لا يعلمون

DOI: 10.4324/9781032658858-4

> So, direct your face [i.e., self] toward the religion, inclining to truth. [adhere to] the fitrah of Allah upon which He has created [all] people. No change should there be in the creation of Allah. That is the correct religion, but most of the people do not know.
>
> (Qur'ân 30:30)

This verse underscores the notion that human beings are naturally inclined towards righteousness and the recognition of a higher power.

Fitrah is a moral compass that guides individuals towards ethical understanding and good behaviour. In addition to recognising *fitrah*, Islāmic teachings emphasise the importance of nurturing and refining one's innate disposition and character through various moral virtues. These virtues include sincerity (*ikhlas*), honesty (*sidq*), patience (*sabr*), humility (*tawadhu'*) and compassion (*rahmah*), among others. Islāmic scholars have elaborated on these virtues and guided how to cultivate them in one's life. Moreover, the Prophet Muhammad (ﷺ) said, "Verily, Allāh does not look at your appearance or wealth, but rather He looks at your hearts and actions" (Al-Qushayri, 2000). This *hādīth* highlights the importance of focusing on inner qualities and intentions rather than outward appearances or material possessions. It encourages individuals to develop a sound and virtuous character rooted in sincerity and righteousness.

Islāmic scholars and psychologists have extensively explored the concept of *fitrah* and its role in moral development. They argue that recognising and nurturing this innate disposition is crucial for developing strong moral character. Islāmic teachings and scholarly works emphasise the significance of *fitrah*. They guide fostering moral growth and contributing to a just and compassionate society. Imam Al-Ghazālī, a renowned Islāmic scholar, emphasises the importance of recognising and cultivating *fitrah* in his works. He asserts that an individual's *fitrah* inclines them to recognise moral truths and differentiate between right and wrong. However, this inclination can be influenced and veiled by harmful external factors and societal influences. To combat this, individuals must strive to develop their *fitrah* by engaging in self-reflection, introspection, and knowledge seeking. This will ensure their *fitrah* remains intact and guide their moral choices towards the correct path (Al-Ghazzali, 2010).

In addition, Islāmic teachings emphasise the significance of moral education and upbringing in shaping an individual's character. Beyond the individual's personal responsibility, parents, educators, and society are responsible for providing a nurturing environment that promotes moral values and ethical behaviour. In the rich tapestry of Islāmic teachings, the emphasis on moral education and upbringing is a cornerstone for developing an individual's character. The Prophet Muhammad (ﷺ) himself is celebrated as the embodiment of exemplary character, and his teachings stress the pivotal role of a virtuous upbringing in shaping the fabric of a righteous society.

Parents are considered the first and foremost educators entrusted with instilling a strong moral compass in their children. Islāmic educational institutions, too, bear the weighty responsibility of imparting academic knowledge and the ethical principles embedded in the teachings of Islām. As society is viewed as a collective entity, its role extends beyond mere observance to active participation in fostering an atmosphere where moral values flourish, creating a harmonious and just community. In this holistic perspective, the teachings of Islām weave a narrative that underscores the interconnectedness of individual character development and the broader societal responsibility towards nurturing ethical conduct. The Prophet Muhammad (ﷺ) said, "Every child is born in a state of *fitrah*, then his parents make him a Jew, a Christian or a Magian (Zoroastrian)" (Al-Bukhari & Khan, 1987). This *hādīth* highlights the role of upbringing and social influences in preserving or distorting one's innate disposition.

Psychologists have also explored the concept of *fitrah* from a developmental perspective. They argue that children are born with an inherent moral sensitivity and a predisposition towards compassion, empathy, and fairness. This moral sensitivity can be observed in young children's behaviour, as they exhibit a natural aversion to injustice and show signs of empathy towards others' distress. Researchers have conducted various studies on young children to investigate the influence of *fitrah* on their moral judgement and behaviour (Damon, 2008; Hoffman, 2001; Krebs, 2011). Furthermore, exploring *fitrah* in developmental psychology sheds light on the intricate interplay between innate moral inclinations and environmental influences.

As psychologists delve into the origins of moral sensitivity, they recognise that while *fitrah* provides a foundational predisposition, environmental factors play a crucial role in shaping the manifestation of these innate qualities. Children's early experiences, cultural context, and social interactions contribute to the nuanced development of their moral compass. Understanding the interdependence of *fitrah* and environmental influences opens avenues for tailored interventions and educational strategies that nurture and reinforce positive moral development in children. This holistic approach acknowledges the synergy between inherent tendencies and external factors, offering a more comprehensive understanding of the intricacies of moral development in the early stages of life (El-Moslimany, 2018; Ma'mun et al., 2023; Narvaez & Lapsley, 2013; Susanto & Hamiyya, 2023).

For instance, in Irshad's (2023) doctoral dissertation titled, *In Search of Understanding the Primordial Human Nature (Fitra): The Encounter of Islāmic Theological, Philosophical, and Mystical Views, and Modern Science*, the author delves into an interdisciplinary exploration of the concept of *fitrah* by examining Islāmic theological, philosophical, and mystical perspectives in conjunction with insights from modern science. This comprehensive investigation sheds light on the intricate intersections between religious and scientific understandings of human nature, offering a nuanced and holistic perspective that contributes to the ongoing dialogue between faith and reason while highlighting the compatibility of Islāmic thought with contemporary scientific knowledge (Irshad, 2023).

In essence, *fitrah*, often translated simply as innate disposition, is every individual's inherent moral compass according to Islāmic belief. The natural understanding of right and wrong is ingrained within each person. Recognising this inherent nature is the first step towards moral development in Islāmic psychology. As individuals strive to align their actions with this natural disposition, they embark on character-building and ethical understanding. Islāmic teachings provide a framework for nurturing and cultivating the virtues associated with *fitrah*, emphasising the importance of honesty, compassion, and justice. By consciously aligning their behaviour with these virtues, individuals strengthen their moral character and contribute to creating a just and compassionate society in line with the broader ethical teachings of Islām.

3.2 The Stages of Moral Development in Islāmic Psychology

Building upon the concept of *fitrah*, we explore the stages of moral development in Islāmic psychology. As in other psychological theories, Islāmic psychology recognises moral reasoning and behaviour progression through distinct stages. We delve into these stages, drawing from Islāmic scripture, traditions, and contemporary psychological research, to comprehensively understand how individuals evolve morally within an Islāmic framework. By examining the moral milestones that individuals pass through, we shed light on the intricate dynamics of moral development and the factors that contribute to its progression. The concept of *fitrah*, inherent goodness or innate predisposition, is the foundation upon which Islāmic psychology builds its understanding of moral development. Expanding beyond the innate nature of individuals, Islāmic psychology acknowledges the dynamic nature of moral growth and outlines various stages in this process.

3.2.1 The Amoral Stage

The first stage of moral development in Islāmic psychology is known as the pre-conventional morality stage or the amoral stage. At this stage, individuals are primarily driven by their basic instincts and desires. They lack a developed sense of right and wrong and are focused on immediate gratification. This stage is similar to Lawrence Kohlberg's pre-conventional stage of moral development (Kohlberg, 1985), where morality and ethical considerations are determined by personal interest and the fear or avoidance of punishment. In the pre-conventional morality stage of Islāmic psychology, individuals navigate a realm where basic instincts and desires shape their moral compass.

In Islāmic psychology, this phase is often called the amoral stage, emphasising the absence of a fully developed sense of right and wrong. At this point, individuals are driven by immediate gratification, seeking to fulfil their basic needs and desires without a profound reflection on the ethical implications of their actions. The emphasis on self-interest aligns with the understanding that individuals are still in the early stages of moral development, gradually evolving towards a more refined and principled approach to ethical decision-making as they progress through subsequent stages. The recognition of this foundational phase underscores the importance of guiding individuals towards a higher moral consciousness within the framework of Islāmic teachings (Curran, 2013; Kaplick & Skinner, 2017; Kohlberg, 1987).

Islāmic teachings stress the importance of instilling empathy, self-control, and compassion in children from a young age to help shape their morals at this critical stage. This is because Islāmic psychology recognises the influence of several social and environmental factors on moral development. These factors include family, community, education, religious teachings, and individual and collective roles in shaping the *fitrah* of evolving children. The family is the primary institution for moral development, and parents are responsible for providing a nurturing and morally conducive environment for their children. Qur'ân 64 verse 15 says:

إنما أموالكم وأولادكم فتنة

Your wealth and your children are but a trial.

This stresses that parents in Islām are responsible for rearing morally upright children. The Prophet Muhammad (ﷺ) also emphasises the responsibility of parents in nurturing children upon Islāmic principles and values in the following *hādīth*, narrated by Abdullah ibn Umar. The Messenger of Allāh (ﷺ) was reported to have said, "Each of you is a shepherd and is responsible for his flock" (Sahih Muslim).

The emphasis on parental guidance and early childhood upbringing in Islām underscores the pivotal role parents play in shaping the moral compass of their children. The teachings of Prophet Muhammad (ﷺ) emphasise the profound responsibility parents bear in fostering an environment rooted in Islāmic principles and values. Beyond imparting religious knowledge, Islāmic teachings highlight the need to instil broader virtues such as empathy, self-control, and compassion during a child's formative years. The Prophet's (ﷺ) teachings serve as a beacon, guiding parents to mould not just the religious identity of their children but also their character and conduct.

Furthermore, the community plays a vital role in shaping individuals' moral values through social interactions and collective norms. Education is also a significant catalyst in the moral development process within Islāmic psychology. In a *hādīth*, the Prophet Muhammad (peace be upon him) was reported to have said, "Seeking knowledge is obligatory upon every Muslim". Schools and educational institutions are seen as compulsory players in the moral development of individuals and society. They are platforms where ethical principles are taught and reinforced through curricular and extracurricular activities. Beyond mainstream schooling, Islāmic education, including Qur'ânic studies and Seerah, provides individuals with a comprehensive understanding of moral values and principles.

Islāmic teachings, deeply embedded in mainstream and Islāmic educational systems, guide individuals towards understanding the importance of virtues such as compassion, justice, and integrity. The study of the Prophet's life (Seerah) supplements these teachings by providing real-life examples of compassion, justice, and empathy. Additionally, religious teachings, such as schooling individuals on the five pillars of Islām (Shahādah, Salāh, Zakāh, Sawm, and Hajj), offer guidance on ethical conduct and moral responsibilities towards oneself and others. The five pillars of Islām, the foundation of ethical conduct, extend beyond personal beliefs to emphasise social and communal obligations.

For instance, *zakāh*, the practice of giving to those in need, highlights the importance of compassion and generosity towards others. Similarly, the emphasis on Salāh, the ritualistic prayers, underscores the significance of self-discipline and spiritual connection. This comprehensive approach to ethical education within the Islāmic framework guides individuals in their personal lives and shapes a community where moral values are upheld collectively, fostering a harmonious and ethically conscious society (Halstead, 2004; Waghid, 2016). The intertwining of religious teachings throughout the educational journey reinforces moral values and ethical conduct, instilling a sense of responsibility and accountability.

In Qur'ân (3:110), Allah says:

كنتم خير أمة أخرجت للناس تأمرون بالمعروف وتنهون عن المنكر وتؤمنون بالله

> You are the best nation produced [as an example] for mankind. You enjoin what is right and forbid what is wrong.
>
> (Ali 'Imran 3,110)

This stresses the Islāmic conviction that any education is incomplete without moral development. Furthermore, Islāmic education not only imparts knowledge about moral values and principles but also instils a sense of responsibility and accountability in individuals. In the holistic perspective of Islāmic psychology, these interconnected factors – family, community, education, and religious teachings – collaborate harmoniously to shape an individual's moral compass, fostering a strong ethical foundation that extends beyond personal behaviour to contribute positively to the broader societal fabric (Lubis, 2015; Rachmawati et al., n.d.; Rusli, 2020).

In Islāmic tradition, the foundation of moral development is laid in early childhood due to the profound impact that teaching children the principles of compassion, integrity, and righteousness can have at such a tender age. This holistic approach to parenting in Islām seeks to cultivate well-rounded individuals who contribute positively to their communities and society. Islāmic researchers such as Arif (2018), Farisia (2020), Musharraf (2015), and Samsinar et al. (2023) have also highlighted the significance of parental guidance and early childhood upbringing in shaping moral development during this stage.

3.2.2 The Heteronomous Stage

The second stage of moral development in Islāmic psychology is known as the conventional morality stage or the heteronomous stage. At this stage, individuals develop a sense of right and wrong based on external authority and societal norms. They conform to these norms and seek approval from others. This stage aligns with Kohlberg's conventional stage of moral development, where morality is determined by adherence to social norms and rules to the point that adherence to these established social norms becomes a guiding principle in moral decision-making. Besides this, the heteronomous stage in Islāmic psychology stresses the development of a strong moral conscience and understanding of the consequences of one's actions.

Umar bin Al-Khattab, a foremost companion of the Prophet Muhammad (ﷺ), also said, "I heard Allāh's Messenger (peace be upon him) saying, "Actions are judged by motives" (Bukhari). This *hādīth* foregrounds the place of intention in moral development and the evolvement of *fitrah*. While the individual at this stage may at first do what is right with the motive of seeking social or parental approval, as they evolve and as the innateness (*fitrah*) of doing good is further instilled, they must begin to think and act morally, not just to escape societal/parental wrath, but because they are gradually being taught to understand the importance of cultivating good virtues.

During the conventional morality stage in Islāmic psychology, individuals navigate the intricacies of ethical understanding within the framework of external authority and societal norms. Islāmic teachings stress the importance of adhering to the collective moral fabric as outlined in the Qur'ân and *hādīth*. During this stage, the individual is moulded by a profound awareness of societal expectations and seeks validation from the community. The emphasis on conformity to established norms reflects the broader Islāmic emphasis on communal harmony and mutual respect. This stage, therefore, becomes a crucial stepping stone in the moral development of individuals, laying the foundation for a sense of responsibility and accountability within the larger societal context.

Furthermore, Islāmic teachings emphasise the importance of following the commandments of Allāh and the guidance of the Prophet Muhammad (ﷺ) as the ultimate source of moral authority. Allāh says in Qur'ân (4:59):

يايها الذين ءامنوا أطيعوا الله وأطيعوا الرسول وأولي الأمر منكم

O you who have believed, obey Allāh and obey the Messenger and those in authority among you.

Muslims are encouraged to live by the dictates of their Lord, his Prophet, and their leaders to direct and further improve their *fitrah*. This includes living according to justice, honesty, and compassion, as exemplified by the Prophet's teachings and actions. This emphasis on following the commandments of Allāh and the guidance of Prophet Muhammad (ﷺ) not only shapes the ethical framework of individual Muslims but also permeates various aspects of their lives, including professional conduct.

Muslim psychologists, in particular, find resonance between their ethical obligations in the field and the moral teachings of Islām. The commitment to justice, honesty, and compassion aligns seamlessly with the ethical principles upheld in psychology. The teachings of the Prophet Muhammad (ﷺ) serve as a guiding light, encouraging psychologists to approach their work with empathy and a sense of responsibility towards the well-being of their clients. In fostering a strong moral conscience, these teachings contribute to a holistic understanding of ethical practice, ensuring that justice and compassion extend beyond personal conduct and into the professional realm.

The synthesis of Islāmic teachings and psychological ethics creates a framework that guides individual behaviour and enriches the therapeutic relationship, reinforcing the importance of moral integrity in the pursuit of psychological well-being. Besides, the fact that Kohlberg's conventional stage aligns with the principles and stages of Islāmic psychology highlights the universal nature of moral development and the common threads that weave through diverse ethical frameworks (Al-Attar, 2010; N. Iqbal & Skinner, 2021; Kohlberg, 1987).

3.2.3 The Autonomous Stage

The third stage of moral development in Islāmic psychology is the post-conventional morality stage or the autonomous stage. At this stage, individuals develop moral principles and act according to internalised values rather than relying solely on external authority. This stage is akin to Kohlberg's post-conventional stage of moral development, where individuals adhere to universal ethical principles and consider the greater good. In the field of Islāmic psychology, the post-conventional morality stage represents a profound level of moral development, where individuals transcend external authority and begin to forge their ethical compass.

Drawing parallels with Kohlberg's post-conventional stage, this phase signifies a departure from rigid adherence to societal norms towards a more autonomous and principled approach to decision-making. In the Islāmic context, individuals at this stage are encouraged to internalise and embrace the universal ethical principles embedded in Islāmic teachings, guided by a deep sense of personal responsibility. This transition underscores a maturation in moral reasoning, emphasising a commitment to principles that transcend cultural or societal constraints. As individuals navigate the complexities of ethical dilemmas at the post-conventional morality stage in Islāmic psychology, they reflect a capacity for independent judgement, moral autonomy, and a profound understanding of the universal principles that underpin Islāmic ethics (Forsyth, 2020; Mustea et al., 2010; Shehu, 1998).

Islāmic teachings urge individuals to strive for the highest moral standards and to engage in critical thinking and reflection. Scholars emphasise the importance of *Ijtihad* (independent reasoning) and *Ihsân* (excellence in conduct) at this stage. The Islāmic belief in human beings' capability for independent reasoning is accentuated in Qur'ân (2:256), where Allah says, "There is no compulsion in religion; the right path has become distinct from the wrong path". The emphasis on *Ijtihad*, or independent reasoning, underscores the importance of critical thinking and intellectual engagement. Muslims are encouraged to memorise and follow traditions and actively seek a profound comprehension of Islāmic principles.

This intellectual endeavour is complemented by ingraining the concept of *Ihsân*, which translates to excellence in conduct, into one's conduct. It implies a holistic approach to practising Islām, encompassing adherence to rules and the cultivation of virtuous character traits. Moreover, Islāmic scholars advocate for applying these principles in contemporary contexts, recognising the dynamic nature of society. Muslims are encouraged to develop a deep understanding of *Ihsân* and other core Islāmic principles and apply them in contemporary contexts while considering the overall objectives (*maqasid*) of Islāmic law. Within the framework of Islāmic teachings, the call for individuals to adhere to the highest moral standards extends beyond mere compliance with legal precepts.

For instance, in a *hādīth* narrated by Aisha (R.A), one of the wives of the Prophet Muhammad (ﷺ), the Prophet (ﷺ) was reported to have said, "Verily, Allāh loves that one should be kind and lenient in all matters" (Sahih Muslim). This *hādīth* stresses that beyond compliance with Islāmic laws and precepts, Muslims must internalise Islāmic principles to the point of being innately kind and lenient, especially at this stage of moral development where external factors no longer determine an individual's actions. A central feature of the autonomous stage is that the pursuit of a deep understanding of Islāmic teachings, coupled with critical thinking and a commitment to moral excellence, empowers individuals to navigate the complexities of the modern world while remaining grounded in the timeless values of Islām (Auda, 2022; Khan & Khan, 2019; Yilmaz, 2003).

To sum up the discussions on the stages of moral development, it is pertinent to stress that Islāmic psychology recognises all the stages (of moral development) that individuals progress through, from the amoral to the heteronomous and, finally, the autonomous stage. For each stage, Islāmic psychology proffers principles and guidelines for helping individuals develop their *fitrah* positively. Exceptionally, Islāmic teachings, including the Qur'ân and the Prophet Muhammad's (ﷺ) traditions, provide guidance and principles that shape moral development within an Islāmic framework. Moreover, the stages outlined in Islāmic psychology align with the broader field of moral development theories, most notably Lawrence Kohlberg's stages of moral development. By understanding the stages and factors (such as family dynamics, community influence, educational experiences, and the teachings of Islām) involved, individuals can work towards developing strong moral character and contributing positively to society based on Islāmic principles. Most importantly, the Islāmic psychological framework emphasises the interplay between the above-listed factors, underscoring the importance of a holistic approach to fostering virtuous character.

3.3 Another Dimension to the Stages of Moral Development

Aside from the Islāmic psychological perspective on moral development, Islāmic religious scholars have also identified several stages of moral development that individuals progress through as they grow and mature. One prominent model is the division of moral development into three stages: the stage of responsibility, the stage of self-purification, and the stage of self-perfection (Al-Ghazzali, 2010). In the intricate tapestry of Islāmic ethics, delineating moral development into three distinct stages provides a roadmap for personal growth. It reflects a profound understanding of human nature within the Islāmic tradition. This multifaceted model not only encapsulates the dynamic nature of moral development within the Islāmic framework but also serves as a guide for individuals navigating the intricate journey towards ethical excellence (Al Haq et al., 2016; Amini, 2014; Madayen et al., 2021). Below is a brief examination of the three stages.

3.3.1 The Stage of Responsibility

The first stage, responsibility, marks the initial awakening of moral consciousness, wherein individuals recognise their duties and obligations towards others. This stage lays the foundation for moral conduct and ethical behaviour and creates a foundational awareness that lays the groundwork for the subsequent stages. The stage of responsibility involves understanding and fulfilling one's duties and obligations towards oneself, family, society, and ultimately, towards Allāh. At its core, this stage transcends the mere acknowledgement of duties; it beckons individuals to delve deep into the profound understanding of their obligations to themselves, their families, society, and, most profoundly, Allāh.

It serves as the bedrock upon which the edifice of moral conduct and ethical behaviour is erected, shaping the contours of a virtuous and principled existence. This journey involves recognising one's responsibilities and actively fulfilling these duties with a sense of conscientious commitment. In the Islāmic context, the concept of responsibility is intricately interwoven with divine guidance, as believers are encouraged to discharge their duties with the consciousness that they are ultimately accountable to Allāh for their actions. Within this framework, individuals navigate life's complexities, striving to strike a harmonious balance between personal fulfilment and societal contributions, all while remaining steadfast in their commitment to a higher purpose.

3.3.2 The Stage of Self-Purification

The stage of self-purification explores deeper, urging individuals to reflect inwardly, purify their intentions, and rectify their actions. It is a transformative phase where self-awareness and accountability intertwine, fostering a sense of spiritual refinement. The stage of self-purification (*tazkiyah an nafs*) focuses on purging one's inner self from negative traits and vices such as greed, envy, and anger. Islāmic teachings emphasise the importance of self-reflection and self-discipline in this stage, as individuals strive to overcome their lower desires and develop virtues such as patience, humility, and gratitude. In the journey of self-purification within Islāmic teachings, the emphasis on cultivating inner virtues extends beyond merely avoiding negative traits. It calls for a profound self-examination and a conscious effort to nurture qualities that elevate the individual spiritually and morally.

Islām encourages believers to engage in regular self-reflection, which involves scrutinising one's thoughts, actions, and intentions with a sincere desire for positive transformation. This introspective practice goes hand in hand with self-discipline as individuals learn to navigate the intricacies of their inner selves, confronting and mitigating the influences of greed, envy, and anger. As the process unfolds, the focus shifts towards the development of virtues like patience, humility, and gratitude. Patience becomes a shield against impulsivity, humility fosters a sense of interconnectedness, and gratitude anchors the individual in appreciation of the blessings around them. Thus, the stage of self-purification becomes a dynamic and transformative journey, guiding individuals towards a more virtuous and spiritually enriched existence (Murad, 2013; Yusuf, 2012).

3.3.3 The Stage of Self-Perfection

Finally, the stage of self-perfection represents the pinnacle of moral maturity, where individuals strive for excellence in their character and conduct, aligning their lives with the ethical teachings of Islām. The stage of self-perfection is characterised by the cultivation of higher moral qualities and the pursuit of excellence. It involves the development of virtues such as justice, mercy, and compassion as individuals strive to emulate the attributes of Allāh and become a source of goodness and benefit to others. In pursuing self-perfection, individuals embark on a transformative journey to embody the highest moral qualities possible and achieve a state of excellence. This stage goes beyond personal development, exploring the area of virtues that align with divine attributes.

Central to this journey is cultivating justice, mercy and compassion, virtues revered in Islāmic teachings. As individuals strive to emulate the benevolent attributes of Allāh, they not only enhance their character but also become a source of goodness and benefit to the broader community. The commitment to justice ensures fairness and equity in all interactions, while mercy and compassion create a nurturing environment that fosters empathy and understanding. In this quest for self-perfection, individuals not only shape their destinies but also contribute positively to the interconnected fabric of society, embodying the essence of virtue and moral excellence (Al-Haddad, 2003; M. Iqbal, 2013; Murata & Chittick, 1996).

3.4 Nurturing Virtuous Character in the Islāmic Tradition

In the Islāmic tradition, nurturing virtuous character is crucial to personal and spiritual development. Islām offers a comprehensive framework encompassing principles, values, and practices to cultivate moral excellence and build strong character. Within the rich amalgam of the Islāmic tradition, cultivating virtuous character emerges as a fundamental cornerstone of personal and spiritual growth.

Islām, as a holistic way of life, goes beyond mere ritualistic practices and explores the intricate nuances of ethical conduct. It provides a comprehensive roadmap for individuals seeking to navigate the terrain of moral excellence. Two main concepts stand out here: *Akhlaq* and *Adab*. The concept of *Akhlaq* (morality) in Islām transcends outward actions, emphasising the internal disposition of the individual. It is a conscious effort to align one's behaviour with the divine principles in the sacred text, the Qur'ân. Similarly, the concept of *Adab* (good manners and etiquette) is also deeply ingrained in Islāmic teachings. Muslims are encouraged to display humility, sweet temperedness, kindness and compassion in their interactions, fostering a sense of community and mutual respect.

Drawing inspiration from the Qur'ân and the teachings of Prophet Muhammad (ﷺ), Islāmic scholars have expounded on the virtues and values that form the bedrock of noble character. These virtues, including humility, kindness, and forgiveness, have been discussed extensively in the previous chapter. Muslims are expected to develop these character traits through prayer, reflection, adherence to ethical principles, and engaging in acts of charity, known as *sadaqah* or *zakāh*. On the one hand, prayer, reflection, and adherence to ethical principles are believed to help individuals in their transformative journey towards the development of virtuous character traits that extend beyond personal growth to positive communal and societal development (Al-Aidaros et al., 2013; Hirschkind, 2006; Ramadan, 2006). On the other hand, *sadaqah* and *zakāh* are seen as means of purifying the soul, cultivating generosity and creating economically and morally empowered societies (Ramadan, 2006).

Another important means of character development is studying the life and teachings of the Prophet Muhammad (ﷺ). Studying the life and teachings of the Prophet Muhammad (ﷺ), his exemplary character and actions create a profound avenue for character development within the Islāmic tradition. His life is a timeless and unparalleled source of inspiration for Muslims seeking to cultivate virtuous qualities. The Prophet's actions and sayings, meticulously documented in *Hādīths*, offer a comprehensive guide on ethical behaviour, compassion, patience, and humility. Exploring the intricacies of his life allows individuals to extract invaluable lessons that resonate across diverse contexts. The Prophet's ability to navigate challenges gracefully, demonstrate kindness, and uphold justice exemplifies a blueprint for ethical conduct (Shah, 2009).

This is why Islāmic scholars commonly refer to his character traits as the "Prophetic Virtues" or "Islāmic Ethical Virtues". As Islāmic educational practices emphasise character-building alongside intellectual development, Muslims are encouraged to cultivate these virtues in their interactions with others, striving to embody the highest standards of moral conduct. Hence, Islāmic schools and institutions often incorporate moral education programs that focus on developing Prophetic virtues and nurturing moral consciousness in students. Such programs aim to instil ethical values and moral responsibility, promoting a holistic approach to education. These Prophetic virtues serve as a moral compass for Muslims, guiding their behaviour in various aspects of life, including professional settings like psychology.

When Muslim psychologists adhere to the principles of sincerity, trustworthiness, and justice, they not only align with the ethical standards of their profession but also integrate the Prophetic virtues into their therapeutic relationships. The emphasis on character development within Islāmic education further reinforces the importance of ethical virtues, encouraging psychologists to go beyond mere adherence to confidentiality rules to actively embody a morally upright demeanour (Al-Karam, 2020; Tan, 2012). In this way, the fusion of psychological ethics with Islāmic virtues profoundly impacts the therapeutic process, fostering an environment where clients feel respected and confidential and guided by a practitioner committed to the highest standards of moral conduct.

To sum up, the Islāmic tradition offers a comprehensive framework for nurturing virtuous character and moral development (Al-Attas, 1995). Central to this framework is the concept of *fitrah*, the inherent and natural disposition towards goodness that every individual possesses. By emphasising the concept of *fitrah*, identifying the stages of moral development from religious and psychological perspectives, and outlining practical guidance on cultivating virtuous character traits, Islām provides individuals, families, and communities with a roadmap for personal and spiritual growth. Through self-reflection, self-discipline, and the emulation of Prophetic virtues, Muslims are encouraged to strive for moral excellence and become agents of positive societal change. Recognising the stages of moral development outlined in Islāmic teachings, individuals are guided through a transformative journey that encompasses ethical values, empathy, and social responsibility.

Islāmic educational practices further reinforce the importance of character-building alongside intellectual development, ensuring a holistic approach to education. The practical guidance embedded in Islāmic teachings encourages Muslims to continuously self-reflect, exercise self-discipline, and emulate the virtuous character traits exemplified by the Prophet Muhammad. This proactive approach to moral growth fosters a sense of responsibility to contribute positively to society, making Muslims beneficiaries of ethical teachings and agents of positive change. Moreover, the integration of character-building practices within Islāmic educational systems ensures that intellectual development is complemented by a deep commitment to moral excellence, creating well-rounded individuals equipped to navigate life with integrity and compassion.

References

Al-Aidaros, A.-H., Mohd Shamsudin, F., & Md Idris, K. (2013). Ethics and ethical theories from an Islāmic perspective. *International Journal of Islāmic Thought*, *4*, 1–13.

Al-Attar, M. (2010). *Islāmic ethics: Divine command theory in Arabo-Islāmic thought*. Routledge.

Al-Attas, M. N. (1995). *Prolegomena to the metaphysics of Islām: An exposition of the fundamental elements of the worldview of Islām*. International Institute of Islāmic Thought and Civilization. https://books.google.com.ng/books?id=NSEqAAAACAAJ

Al-Bukhari, M. I. B. N. I., & Khan, M. M. (1987). *The translation of the meanings of Sahih Al-bukhari: Arabic-English* (Issue v. 4). Kitab Bhavan. https://books.google.com.ng/books?id=F6rtwAEACAAJ

Al-Ghazzali. (2010). *The alchemy of happiness*. Cosimo Classics. https://books.google.com.ng/books?id=htx2zqa0TNkC

Al-Haddad, I. A. I. (2003). The book of assistance (M. Badawi, Trans.). Fons Vitae.

Al Haq, M. A., Abdul Ghani, A., & Ahmad, N. H. (2016). Islāmic prayer, spirituality and productivity: An exploratory conceptual analysis. *Al-Iqtishad: Journal of Islāmic Economics*, *8*(2), 271–286.

Al-Karam, C. Y. (2020). Islāmic psychology: Expanding beyond the clinic. *Journal of Islāmic Faith and Practice*, *3*(1), 111–120.
Al-Qushayri, M. H. (2000). *The translation of the meanings of summarized Sahih Muslim: Arabic-English: Vol. 2*. Darussalam. https://books.google.com.ng/books?id=aiGxDcQTsysC
Amini, A. I. (2014). *Self building*. Lulu. com.
Arif, S. (2018). *Ghazali's personality theory: A study on the importance of humility in early childhood*. Ibn Haldun University, Alliance of Civilization Institute.
Auda, J. (2022). *Maqasid al-Shari'ah as philosophy of Islāmic law*. International Institute of Islāmic Thought (IIIT).
Curran, C. E. (2013). *The development of moral theology: Five strands*. Georgetown University Press.
Damon, W. (2008). *Moral child: Nurturing children's natural moral growth*. Simon and Schuster.
El-Moslimany, A. (2018). *Teaching children: A moral, spiritual, and holistic approach to educational development*. International Institute of Islāmic Thought (IIIT).
Farisia, H. (2020). Nurturing religious and moral values at early childhood education. *Didaktika Religia*, *8*(1), 1–27.
Forsyth, D. (2020). *Making moral judgments: Psychological perspectives on morality, ethics, and decision-making*. Taylor & Francis.
Halstead, M. (2004). An Islāmic concept of education. In *Comparative education* (Vol. 40, Issue 4, pp. 517–529). https://doi.org/10.1080/0305006042000284510
Hirschkind, C. (2006). The ethical soundscape: Cassette sermons and Islāmic counterpublics. *The Ethical Soundscape: Cassette Sermons and Islāmic Counterpublics*, *15*(2), 32–143. https://doi.org/10.1353/sof.0.0026
Hoffman, M. L. (2001). *Empathy and moral development: Implications for caring and justice*. Cambridge University Press.
Iqbal, M. (2013). *The reconstruction of religious thought in Islām*. Stanford University Press.
Iqbal, N., & Skinner, R. (2021). Islāmic psychology: Emergence and current challenges. *Archive for the Psychology of Religion*, *43*(1), 65–77.
Irshad, A. (2023). *In search of understanding the primordial human nature (Fitra): The encounter of Islāmic theological, philosophical, and mystical views, and modern science*. The George Washington University.
Kaplick, P. M., & Skinner, R. (2017). The evolving Islām and psychology movement. *European Psychologist*, *22*(3), 198–204.
Khan, M. A. M., & Khan, M. A. M. (2019). Ihsan: Classical and contemporary understanding. In *Islām and good governance: A Political Philosophy of Ihsan* (pp. 77–102). Palgrave Macmillan, New York. https://doi.org/10.1057/978-1-137-54832-0_4
Kohlberg, L. (1985) Kohlberg's stages of moral development. In W. C. Crain (Ed.), *Theories of development* (pp. 118–136). Prentice-Hall.
Kohlberg, L. (1987). The psychology of moral development. *Ethics*, *97*(2).
Krebs, D. (2011). *The origins of morality: An evolutionary account*. Oxford University Press.
Lubis, M. A. (2015). Effective implementation of the integrated Islāmic education. *Global Journal Al-Thaqafah*, *5*(1), 59–68.

Ma'mun, S., Usmani, S. A. A., & Maliki, I. A. (2023). The childfree phenomenon among urban Muslims: A multidisciplinary examination of science and morality. *Akademika: Jurnal Pemikiran Islām*, *28*(1), 111–126.

Madayen, S. M. A., Seif-Farshad, M., & Kheire, Y. (2021). Investigating the compatibility of Mulla Sadra's ethics with the three schools of normative. *International Journal of Multicultural and Multireligious Understanding*, *8*(11), 84–95.

Murad, K. (2013). *In the early hours: Reflections on spiritual and self development*. Kube Publishing Ltd.

Murata, S., & Chittick, W. C. (1996). *The vision of Islām: The foundations of Muslim faith and practice*. I. B. Tauris. https://books.google.com.ng/books?id=j2EwAAAAYAAJ

Musharraf, M. N. (2015). Islāmic education in Europe-A comprehensive analysis. *Australian Journal of Humanities and Islāmic Studies Research (AJHISR)*, *1*(1), 6–13.

Mustea, A., Negru, O., & Opre, A. (2010). Morality and religion: A psychological perspective. *Journal for the Study of Religions and Ideologies*, *9*(26), 18–35.

Narvaez, D., & Lapsley, D. (2013). Becoming a moral person – Moral development and moral character education as a result of social interactions. In *Empirically informed ethics: Morality between facts and norms* (pp. 227–238). Springer.

Rachmawati, D. E., Ardani, A. N., & Sapitri, R. P. (n.d.). *Moral foundation in psychology and Islāmic perspective*. ICONIPSY Proceedings 2022, 2(1), 2580, 26.

Ramadan, T. (2006). *In the footsteps of the prophet: Lessons from the life of muhammad*. Oxford University Press. https://books.google.com.my/books?id=wW2x_iaqKZgC

Rusli, R. (2020). The role of family in preventing social conflict in society from Islāmic perspectives. *Hunafa: Jurnal Studia Islāmika*, *17*(1), 108–122.

Samsinar, S., Fatimah, F., Syamsuddin, A., & Dewantara, A. H. (2023). Character development model for early childhood learners at Islāmic kindergarten. *Didaktika: Jurnal Kependidikan*, *17*(1), 43–57.

Shah, M. (2009). *The hādīth: Articulating the beliefs and constructs of classical Islām*. Routledge.

Shehu, S. (1998). Toward an Islāmic perspective of developmental psychology. *American Journal of Islām and Society*, *15*(4), 41–70.

Susanto, S., & Hamiyya, I. R. (2023). Organizing the humanistic curriculum with the concept of Fitrah-Based Education. *INTEGRATIA: Journal of Education, Human Development, and Community Engagement*, *1*(1), 1–19.

Tan, C. (2012). *Islāmic education and indoctrination: The case in Indonesia* (Vol. 58). Routledge.

Waghid, Y. (2016). Islāmic education and contemporary ethical dilemmas. In *Oxford research encyclopedia of education*. Oxford University Press.

Yilmaz, I. (2003). Ijtihad and tajdid by conduct. In *Turkish Islām and the secular state, the Gülen movement*. Syracuse University Press, Google Scholar.

Yusuf, H. (2012). *Purification of the heart: Signs, symptoms and cures of the spiritual diseases of the heart*. eBooks2go, Inc.

Part II

Applying Islāmic Ethics in Psychological Practice

4 Ethical Dilemmas and Challenges in Islāmic Psychology

4.0 Introduction

The intricate interplay between culture, spirituality, and mental health has sparked a deeper understanding of the human psyche within the Islāmic framework. In exploring the intersection of Islāmic principles and psychology, the burgeoning field of Islāmic Psychology emerges as a dynamic and nuanced discipline. However, as the synthesis between Islām and psychology unfolds, it brings to the forefront a set of ethical challenges that necessitate careful consideration. A foremost challenge is that secular ethical frameworks have traditionally guided psychology. Grounded in these secular values, psychology often induces distinctive ethical challenges when navigated within religious diversity. As a result, ethical considerations hold paramount importance, and the domain of Islāmic psychology is no stranger to practitioners' nuanced challenges.

When working with Muslim clients, psychologists may encounter unique ethical challenges due to the intersection of religious beliefs and psychological practice. Negotiating the landscape of these ethical dilemmas becomes an inherent part of the professional journey for mental health professionals. This chapter, situated within the broader exploration of applying Islāmic ethics in psychological practice, seeks to dissect the ethical dilemmas and complexities inherent in this unique intersection, offering insights into the challenges faced and proposing thoughtful approaches for ethically sound decision-making in Islāmic Psychology. Moreover, as practitioners engage with Muslim clients, the clash and integration of these two ethical paradigms become evident. This chapter not only dissects the ethical dilemmas arising from this intersection but also delves into the delicate task of addressing religious identity within the context of mental health.

4.1 Balancing Secular and Islāmic Ethical Frameworks: Some Ethical Considerations

The fusion of Islām and psychology acknowledges the profound impact of cultural and spiritual dimensions on mental health, recognising that psychological well-being cannot be divorced from the broader socio-religious

DOI: 10.4324/9781032658858-6

context. However, because psychology is generally rooted in secular principles such as autonomy, beneficence, non-maleficence, and justice, a fusion of Islāmic and mainstream psychology requires careful consideration. These widely accepted principles are the foundation for ethical guidelines and codes of conduct in psychological practice across various countries and organisations (Association, 2016). The principles, regarded as universal ethical pillars, have provided a comprehensive guide for psychologists worldwide. However, when working within an Islāmic context, these frameworks need to be critically examined and harmonised with Islāmic ethical principles to ensure congruence and avoid conflicts.

Delving into the intricacies of cultural and religious contexts, such as within Islāmic societies, demands a nuanced approach. In the Islāmic framework, the ethical landscape is shaped by principles deeply rooted in Islāmic teachings and values. To foster a seamless integration of psychological practices within this context, it becomes imperative to scrutinise and, if necessary, adapt existing frameworks to align with Islāmic ethical principles. This harmonisation process ensures that the psychological interventions not only meet universal ethical standards but also resonate with the specific cultural and religious values of the individuals seeking assistance (Elzamzamy & Keshavarzi, 2019; Haque et al., 2016; Hashim & Rossidy, 2000).

For instance, Islāmic ethical principles, rooted in the Qur'ân and the *Sunnah* (Prophetic traditions), offer a different perspective on morality and guide Muslims in making ethical decisions. Islāmic ethics emphasise the pursuit of moral excellence and the well-being of individuals and society. Key principles in Islāmic ethics include justice, compassion, beneficence, and non-maleficence (Al-Attas, 1989). These principles provide a comprehensive framework for ethical decision-making in all aspects of life, including psychological practice. However, they may also offer contradictory perspectives on clients' mental health issues, hence the challenges that mental health professionals in Islāmic contexts face when attempting to integrate secular and Islāmic ethical frameworks. As we delve into the realm of Islāmic Psychology, it becomes imperative to confront and navigate these ethical dilemmas. Some prominent ethical challenges and considerations are examined in this section.

4.1.1 Autonomy

One of the key challenges is the potential clash between the emphasis on autonomy in secular frameworks and the Islāmic emphasis on divine guidance and submission to Allāh's will. For example, the concept of informed consent may be viewed differently within an Islāmic framework, where communal well-being is prioritised over individual autonomy, resulting in a case-by-case analysis of the society's needs as against a patient's autonomy (Rassool, 2015; Sabry & Vohra, 2013; Saged et al., 2020). Navigating the intersection of secular and Islāmic ethical frameworks in mental health practice requires a delicate balance. It also necessitates a great deal of expertise on the part of the practitioner and trust in the psychologist's expertise and intentions on the patient's part (Hodge, 2018; Kehoe, 2016; Khaleefah, 2022). Moreover, the rich tapestry of Islāmic ethics, woven with threads of justice, compassion, beneficence, non-maleficence, and respect for autonomy, serves as a guiding light for practitioners, offering valuable insights for informed decision-making.

4.1.2 Confidentiality

Another challenge is the potential clash between the value of confidentiality in secular frameworks and the Islāmic emphasis on community and social responsibility. Confidentiality is a fundamental principle in psychotherapy and counselling. In psychology, preserving confidentiality is paramount for fostering trust and creating a safe space for individuals to explore their thoughts and emotions. Islāmic ethics also emphasises the importance of confidentiality in the following verse of the Qur'ân:

إن الله يأمر بالعدل والإحسان وإيتاء ذي القربى

"Indeed, Allah orders justice and good conduct and giving to relatives".

(Qur'ân 16:90)

The verse implies the obligation to protect the privacy and well-being of others. Confidentiality, whose basis lies in justice, fairness, and goodness, is enjoined on all Muslims.

However, while secular psychology frameworks emphasise confidentiality without hammering on boundaries where it should not apply, Islāmic ethical frameworks acknowledge exceptions to confidentiality in certain situations. For instance, if the client poses a risk to themselves or others, or there is a legal obligation to disclose information, the practitioner may breach confidentiality (Leach & Akhurst, 2023). Islāmic ethics also emphasise the importance of seeking advice from knowledgeable individuals and involving family members in mental health therapy when necessary (Baasher, 2001; Mehraki & Gholami, 2017). In Islāmic psychology, it is believed that seeking counsel from wise individuals may offer much-needed insights into the injunctions of Allāh and His Prophet (ﷺ) on the issues troubling the patient. In the same vein, speaking to family members when necessary may provide contextual information on how the issues began, and what the individuals around the patient and their cultural background have contributed to worsening or resolving the issue.

4.1.3 Informed Consent

Informed consent is a vital ethical requirement in psychotherapy and counselling. It has legal, ethical, and clinical implications for patient care. Both secular and Islāmic frameworks place a premium on ensuring that clients have sufficient information to make autonomous decisions about all activities involved in their treatment. Nonetheless, in the Islāmic context, informed consent must align with the principles of Islāmic ethics, emphasising the right to self-determination and the well-being of both the individual and the community. Islāmic teachings emphasise the importance of consent in matters relating to personal autonomy and religious beliefs/obligations.

The Prophet Muhammad (ﷺ) said, "There should be no harm nor reciprocating harm" (Sunan Ibn Majah). This *hādīth* underscores the principle of avoiding harm to others, including withholding information that may negatively impact the client's well-being. This includes patients' right to know what would be done about the information they release to their therapists and the procedures or drugs used in their treatment. These procedures and drugs, for instance, must align with the dictates of patients' religions. Essentially, the Islāmic stance on informed consent in psychotherapy is that practitioners must ensure that clients are fully informed about the nature, risks, and benefits of the therapeutic interventions to be used in their treatment, and the interventions must be done while respecting their cultural and religious beliefs (Leach & Akhurst, 2023).

4.1.4 Ethical Boundaries

Maintaining appropriate boundaries in professional relationships is crucial to ensuring ethical practice. In both the secular and the Islāmic approaches to psychology, psychotherapy is relationship-based, and this means ethical boundaries must be set because the nature of therapist-patient relationships has important clinical and ethical implications for patients' mental health. Psychotherapists are expected to conduct themselves in ways that would not jeopardise their patients' therapeutic process. This includes avoiding sexual relationships with patients and being conscious of the implications of touching, meeting at specific times of the day or locations, giving gifts, etc., in the patient's religious and cultural worldviews. The impact of such practices (i.e., touching, giving gifts, self-disclosure, etc.) on patients' therapeutic journeys must also be considered given the unique experiences that led to their mental health challenges. Similarly, psychotherapists should avoid dual relationships, such as personal friendships or business arrangements with clients.

In light of this, Islāmic ethics emphasises the importance of maintaining modesty, dignity and respect in interactions. Allāh says:

قل للمؤمنين يغضوا من أبصارهم ويحفظوا فروجهم.

Tell the believing men to reduce [some] of their vision and guard their private parts.

(Qur'ân 24:30, Surah An-Nur)

This verse highlights the Islāmic emphasis on modesty and respectful conduct. It is from these virtues that an ideal therapist-patient relationship, free of unethical behaviours, springs. Practitioners must be mindful of establishing and maintaining appropriate boundaries and refrain from engaging in any behaviour that may compromise patients' religious or cultural beliefs and, in the long run, the therapeutic relationship.

For instance, we consider the boundary of touch. On the one hand, secular approaches are not against therapists using non-sexual touch as a medium of connecting and showing solidarity with patients, regardless of gender differences, albeit with the approval of the patient. On the other hand, touch between unrelated members of the opposite sex is expressly forbidden in Islām. As such, a male psychotherapist treating a Muslim female patient (or vice versa) must avoid any physical contact with her as it is considered a sin in Islām for her to touch or be touched by a *non-Mahram*; that is someone she does not have a blood or marital relationship with. All unethical relationships undermining objectivity, professional judgement, and religious obligations/beliefs must be avoided in the Islāmic psychotherapy context.

From the foregoing discussions, it is clear that striking an equilibrium in honouring both secular and Islāmic perspectives demands a thoughtful and culturally sensitive approach. Therapists may grapple with the ethical dilemma of preserving individual privacy while recognising the communal fabric that plays a pivotal role in the Islāmic worldview (Cucchi, 2022). Despite these challenges, Hamza Yusuf and Tariq Ramadan highlight the importance of integrating Islāmic ethical frameworks into psychological practice. They argue that by incorporating Islāmic principles such as preserving life (*hifz al-nafs*), promoting mental well-being (*af'aal al-nafs*), and encouraging moral responsibility (*taklif*), psychologists can provide culturally sensitive and spiritually informed care (Muhammad The Merciful, 2023; Ramadan, 2009, 2013; Yusuf, 2012).

For instance, a Muslim client may seek therapy for depression and express guilt over taking medication due to a belief that relying on medication indicates a lack of trust in God's healing power. The psychologist, guided by both secular and Islāmic ethical principles, acknowledges the client's religious beliefs and collaboratively works with them to address their concerns. The psychologist ensures informed consent, educates the client about the potential benefits of medication in conjunction with therapy, and emphasises that seeking medical help is not contradictory to relying on God's guidance. This reassurance is crucial because religious identity plays a significant role in the lives of many Muslims and can influence their mental health and well-being. Psychologists must recognise and respect Muslims' religious identity as an integral aspect of their overall identity. This requires understanding the diverse ways in which Islām is practised and how it shapes individuals' beliefs, values, and behaviours.

Acknowledging and respecting religious identity is paramount in fostering a holistic approach to mental health care. By recognising the profound impact of religious beliefs on individuals, psychologists can also create a more inclusive and culturally competent therapeutic environment. Furthermore, understanding the diverse spectrum of Islāmic practices allows practitioners to tailor interventions that align with their Muslim clients' unique values and perspectives. This nuanced understanding not only enriches the therapeutic process but also helps address the intricate interplay between religious identity and mental health for a more comprehensive and effective approach to psychological care. It opens avenues for meaningful conversations about spirituality and faith, fostering a collaborative therapeutic relationship. With a comprehensive understanding of Islāmic perspectives on psychological values, psychologists can promote mental well-being by integrating religious identity into the broader context of the individual psychological landscape.

Research conducted by scholars like Amber Haque, Memoona Hasnain, and Maya Hammoud emphasises the need for therapists to have cultural competence and religious literacy when working with Muslim clients (Hammoud et al., 2005; Haque et al., 2016; Hasnain et al., 2011). For instance, a Muslim adolescent struggling with anxiety may want to seek therapy but feels conflicted between religious obligations and social expectations. The psychologist, well-versed in Islāmic teachings and knowledgeable about cultural factors, explores the client's concerns through a religious-cum-cultural lens. They provide a space for the client to express their fears and collaboratively work towards finding a balance between their religious practices and personal goals.

Similarly, psychotherapy and counselling involve intimate conversations and the exploration of deeply personal issues. When working with Muslim clients, psychologists must be mindful of ethical considerations related to confidentiality, boundaries, and potential conflicts between religious and professional duties. Islāmic ethical principles, such as maintaining confidentiality (*sirr*) and upholding trust (*amānah*), align with the core principles of psychotherapy. However, additional considerations arise when dealing with issues such as disclosing sensitive religious information, managing potential conflicts between professional obligations and religious beliefs, and addressing religiously motivated harm (e.g., spiritual abuse).

Scholars highlight the importance of understanding the complexities of religious-based ethical concerns and addressing them in therapeutic settings (Dardas et al., 2016; Fares et al., 2021; Tanios et al., 2009). Practitioners should be aware of the potential for power imbalances in therapy and ensure they do not exploit their position or impose their own religious beliefs on clients. For instance, a Muslim client discloses experiencing spiritual abuse within their religious community and may seek therapy to address the trauma. The psychologist must recognise the importance of addressing the religious aspect of the client's experiences while providing a safe and non-judgemental space. They must validate the client's feelings, help them process the trauma, and collaborate to explore ways to heal while respecting their religious beliefs.

To navigate the challenges and dilemmas that arise in integrating secular and Islāmic ethical frameworks, mental health professionals can employ several strategies discussed in Section 4.3.

4.2 Working with Religious Identity and Mental Health

Religious identity plays a pivotal role in the lives of many individuals, shaping their beliefs, values, and behaviours. When it comes to seeking psychological support, clients with a strong religious affiliation often bring their religious beliefs and practices into the therapeutic setting. This intersection of religious identity and mental health can present unique challenges for practitioners in Islāmic psychology. In the intricate tapestry of human experience, the intersection of religious identity and mental health introduces a nuanced dimension to the therapeutic landscape, particularly in the context of Islāmic psychology. Navigating this delicate terrain requires practitioners to be attuned to the intricate dance between cultural competence and the individual's deeply rooted religious beliefs.

The challenge lies not only in acknowledging the profound impact of faith on the therapeutic process but also in fostering an environment that embraces religious inclusivity without compromising the professionalism and ethical boundaries integral to the therapeutic relationship. As practitioners delve into the realm where spirituality converges with psychology, a profound understanding of the client's religious identity becomes paramount. This exploration not only sheds light on the unique challenges faced by individuals with a strong religious affiliation but also unveils opportunities for therapists to foster a holistic approach that respects and integrates the spiritual dimensions of their clients' lives. In essence, the practice of Islāmic psychology becomes a delicate art, requiring therapists to navigate the fine balance between cultural sensitivity, religious inclusivity, and the integrity of the therapeutic relationship (Abu Raiya & Pargament, 2010; Alqahtani & Altamimi, 2016; Tanhan, 2019). Each of these is discussed below.

4.2.1 Cultural Competence

For one, cultural competence is essential for practitioners working with diverse populations, including those with strong religious identities. To effectively address the needs of clients, practitioners must develop an understanding of their clients' religious backgrounds, traditions, and values. This knowledge allows practitioners to appreciate the significance of religious beliefs in clients' lives and tailor interventions accordingly. Furthermore, cultural competence helps avoid potential misunderstandings, stereotypes, and biases that may arise from unfamiliarity with particular religious traditions. In essence, cultural competence serves as the bridge that connects practitioners with the diverse tapestry of human experience. When working with individuals holding strong religious identities, this competency takes on profound significance. It involves a commitment to delving into the intricate layers of religious backgrounds, traditions, and values that shape the perspectives of clients.

Through this exploration, practitioners gain a nuanced understanding of the profound impact that religious beliefs have on the lives of those they serve. Armed with this awareness, interventions can be finely tuned to resonate with the core values and spiritual dimensions of each individual, fostering a more empathetic and effective therapeutic alliance. Beyond the therapeutic realm, cultural competence acts as a shield against potential pitfalls – shielding against misunderstandings, stereotypes, and biases that might emerge in the absence of familiarity with particular religious traditions. It thus becomes an indispensable tool for building authentic connections and promoting holistic well-being within the diverse mosaic of humanity (Bhui et al., 2007; Hanrahan, 2010; Vieten & Lukoff, 2022).

4.2.2 Religious Inclusivity

One of the primary challenges in working with religious identity and mental health is the potential conflict between religious beliefs and psychological concepts or interventions. Some psychological theories or techniques may be perceived as incompatible or contradictory to religious teachings, leading to resistance or apprehension from clients. For instance, certain therapeutic approaches may encourage self-reflection, questioning religious beliefs or challenging traditional norms, which can be perceived as a threat to religious identity by devout individuals. Practitioners must navigate this delicate balance by respecting clients' religious convictions while integrating appropriate psychological interventions. Navigating the intersection of religious identity and mental health requires practitioners to delicately navigate the potential clash between psychological theories and religious beliefs.

The challenge lies in the approach to addressing the tension that arises when therapeutic techniques clash with deeply held religious convictions. For devout individuals, the fear of compromising their religious identity can lead to resistance or hesitancy in engaging with certain psychological interventions. Successful practitioners recognise the importance of acknowledging and respecting clients' religious beliefs, creating a space where both psychological and spiritual dimensions can coexist harmoniously (Aten & Leach, 2009; Pargament, 2011; Richards & Bergin, 2004).

An essential aspect of working with religious identity and mental health is understanding the impact of religious beliefs on clients' psychological well-being. Research suggests that religious beliefs and practices can have a positive influence on mental health outcomes. For example, studies have found that religious involvement is associated with lower rates of depression, anxiety, and substance abuse (Koenig et al., 2023; Smith et al., 2003). Religious practices, such as prayer or seeking spiritual guidance, can provide individuals with a sense of meaning, hope, and social support, which can contribute to their psychological resilience and coping mechanisms. Furthermore, recognising that individuals draw strength and solace from their religious beliefs, mental health professionals can integrate both secular and religious dimensions into treatment plans to foster holistic well-being.

Nonetheless, it is crucial to recognise that religious beliefs can also pose challenges and contribute to psychological distress. Religious guilt, conflicts between religious teachings and personal desires or pressure to conform to religious expectations can all impact mental health negatively. Practitioners need to be sensitive to these dynamics and provide a safe space for clients to explore and reconcile their religious beliefs with their psychological well-being. Navigating the intersection between religious beliefs and mental health requires a nuanced approach that acknowledges both the positive and potentially challenging aspects of spirituality. While religion can be a source of solace and meaning, it is essential to recognise that individuals may grapple with religious guilt, internal conflicts, or external pressures that can lead to psychological distress. The delicate balance lies in creating a therapeutic environment where clients feel free to explore and reconcile their religious beliefs with their mental well-being without judgement. Practitioners must be attuned to the unique struggles that may arise from the clash between religious teachings and personal desires, offering support and guidance as individuals navigate this intricate terrain (Currier et al., 2023).

4.2.3 Maintaining the Integrity of the Therapeutic Relationship

In promoting religious inclusivity while upholding professional boundaries, practitioners should prioritise the autonomy and well-being of their clients. Islāmic ethical frameworks provide valuable guidance in navigating these complex dynamics while maintaining the integrity of the therapist-patient relationship. Drawing upon Islāmic ethical frameworks can offer profound insights into navigating these intricate dynamics. The principles of privacy (*sirah*) and confidentiality (*sitr*) are essential components of Islāmic ethics and underscore the importance of respecting clients' privacy and safeguarding their sensitive information (Sachedina, 2009). Practitioners should ensure that clients' religious beliefs and practices are treated with dignity and confidentiality, fostering an environment of trust and respect.

Islāmic ethics also emphasise the importance of beneficence (*Ihsân*) and non-maleficence (*la darar*). Practitioners should strive to promote the well-being of their clients and avoid causing harm. This requires a careful assessment of the potential impact of psychological interventions on clients' religious identity and a willingness to adapt therapeutic techniques to align with religious values. Collaborative goal-setting with clients, in which they actively participate in determining treatment objectives, can help ensure that interventions are congruent with their religious beliefs and practices.

Furthermore, fostering a healthy therapeutic relationship requires aligning psychotherapy with the Islāmic principle of justice (*'adl*).

Practitioners should aim to provide equitable and fair treatment to all clients, regardless of their religious background. This involves acknowledging and addressing potential biases or prejudices that may arise from personal beliefs or cultural conditioning. Practitioners must engage in ongoing self-reflection and seek supervision or consultation when faced with ethical dilemmas related to religious identity and mental health. Essentially, practitioners must not only aim to enhance the well-being of their clients but also strive for fairness and equity in their therapeutic approach. Recognising the diversity of religious backgrounds among clients, practitioners are tasked with a careful examination and handling of potential biases and prejudices rooted in personal beliefs or cultural conditioning. The concept of cultural competence extends beyond religious considerations to encompass a broader understanding of diverse cultural backgrounds, fostering an environment where every client is treated with respect and impartiality. To underscore their commitment to providing ethical and culturally sensitive care, practitioners must engage in continuous self-reflection and seeking supervision or consultation (Abu Raiya & Pargament, 2010). This ensures that their interventions are free from personal biases and align with the principles of justice inherent in Islāmic ethics.

4.2.4 Working with Religious Identity and Mental Health: A Case Study

As earlier stated, working with religious identity and mental health in Islāmic psychology presents unique challenges for practitioners, and it is only through a collaborative and respectful approach that practitioners can provide inclusive and tailored care that honours clients' religious identity while promoting their psychological well-being. To illustrate the practical application of these principles, a case study involving a Muslim client experiencing religiously related anxiety can be examined. In this case study, the application of culturally competent principles to relating with a Muslim client grappling with religiously related anxiety becomes crucial for effective intervention.

The practitioner's initial step involves delving into the intricacies of the client's religious background, understanding their beliefs, and acknowledging the profound influence of Islāmic teachings on their overall well-being. Approaching the situation with cultural sensitivity, the practitioner collaborates with the client to devise a treatment plan that seamlessly integrates psychological interventions, all while respecting and incorporating the client's religious convictions. This may manifest through the inclusion of specific religious practices, such as mindfulness or the recitation of relevant verses, as therapeutic coping mechanisms. The practitioner also explores Islāmic teachings on finding tranquillity and entrusting worries to a higher power, tailoring the treatment to align with the client's faith. By doing all these, the practitioner carefully navigates the intersection of religious identity and mental health within the realm of Islāmic psychology, adhering to both psychology and Islāmic ethical frameworks (AbdAllāh Rothman, 2018; Miller, 2003; Rothman & Coyle, 2018).

4.3 Further Insights on Dealing with the Secular-Islāmic Divergence in Islāmic Psychology

Integrating both – that is, secular and Islāmic ethical frameworks in psychological practice – is essential for ensuring all-encompassing therapeutic care for Muslim clients. To this end, this section is an appraisal of ethical procedures and solutions that Muslim psychologists should adopt.

4.3.1 Understanding of Islāmic Ethics and Psychology

First and foremost, practitioners must have a solid understanding of both frameworks and their underlying principles. This knowledge will help practitioners identify areas of congruence and potential conflicts, enabling them to make informed decisions. The addition of a comprehensive understanding of secular and Islāmic ethical frameworks to the conscious cultivation of cultural competence and religious sensitivity will help mental health professionals strengthen the Islāmic psychotherapy process. Moreover, developing a keen awareness of the cultural nuances and diverse perspectives within the Islāmic community allows practitioners to approach their work with a more nuanced and inclusive mindset. Essentially, Islāmic psychotherapists must understand that even among Muslim clients, religious perspectives will differ, and so will the appropriate approach to handling various Muslim clients.

4.3.2 Continuous Professional Development

Second, mental health professionals should engage in ongoing professional development and seek guidance from scholars and experts in Islāmic ethics. This will help deepen their understanding of the Islāmic ethical perspective and provide them with the necessary tools to navigate complex ethical situations. Consulting with Islāmic scholars can be particularly helpful when dealing with unique cases or situations that require a deeper understanding of Islāmic teachings. In addition to this, active engagement with the community and ongoing education about the evolving nature of ethical considerations in both secular and Islāmic contexts is crucial. This continuous learning process ensures that mental health professionals stay attuned to the dynamic nature of ethical standards, facilitating effective and culturally sensitive interventions (Delphin & Rowe, 2008; Plante, 2007; Wise et al., 2010). Continuous learning and open dialogue with clients about their cultural and religious perspectives contribute to a collaborative and culturally sensitive mental health practice (Keshavarzi & Haque, 2013; Malek, 2020; Siegel et al., 2011).

4.3.3 Aligning Ethical Practices with a Balance of both Frameworks

Mental health professionals should engage in reflective practice and engage in regular self-assessment to ensure that their decisions align with both secular and Islāmic ethical frameworks. Supervision and peer support can also play a vital role in this process, providing opportunities for consultation and ethical discussions with colleagues.

4.3.4 Making Ethical Decisions with Religious and Cultural Competence

Asides from understanding variations in religious perspectives, practitioners must also understand the diverse cultural backgrounds of their clients, including how these cultural variations within the Islāmic community colour each client's worldview. This involves not only a broad understanding of Islāmic ethics but also an awareness of the cultural nuances that shape individuals' beliefs and practices. Knowing this is essential when making ethical decisions, as it empowers practitioners to provide effective and respectful care. This is because cultural competence ensures that mental health professionals can tailor their approaches to meet the unique needs of each client, fostering a more inclusive and supportive therapeutic environment. Cultural and religious ethical considerations play crucial roles in the field of psychotherapy and counselling, ensuring the well-being and rights of clients. A case study highlighting the significance of ethical considerations in Islāmic psychology involves a Muslim client seeking counselling for marital issues. The client expresses concern about confidentiality, as disclosure of their problems may lead to social stigma within their community. The practitioner, applying both professional ethics and Islāmic principles, ensures the client's confidentiality by taking necessary precautions to protect their identity and providing reassurance about maintaining privacy. In addition, the practitioner obtains informed consent by thoroughly explaining the counselling process, the potential benefits and the risks involved. They also discuss any cultural or religious factors that may influence the client's decision-making. The practitioner respects the client's autonomy and religious beliefs, allowing them to make informed choices regarding the therapeutic interventions suggested. Furthermore, the practitioner establishes and maintains appropriate boundaries in the therapeutic relationship. They maintain a professional demeanour, refraining from engaging in any behaviour that may be deemed inappropriate or compromising. They remain focused on the client's well-being and address any potential transgressions promptly and ethically (Rothman & Coyle, 2020).

4.3.5 Inculcating Islāmic Ethical Principles

Islāmic ethical frameworks provide valuable guidance for practitioners in navigating ethical dilemmas. Scholars in Islāmic ethics have developed comprehensive frameworks that integrate Islāmic principles with contemporary ethical considerations. These frameworks include principles that facilitate ethical decision-making and shape the professional conduct of Muslim psychologists. For instance, the concept of *maqasid al-shariah*, which focuses on the objectives of Islāmic law, can guide practitioners in balancing the well-being of clients with adherence to Islāmic values. Additionally, excellence (*Ihsân*) highlights the importance of fairness and moral excellence in therapeutic practice (Al-Qaradawi, 2013). This principle (*Ihsân*) is particularly essential as it encourages Muslims to act with excellence of character and sincerity in all aspects of life. Muslim psychologists are enjoined to provide high-quality care, showing compassion, empathy, and professionalism. They should strive to create a therapeutic environment that is conducive to healing and growth, reflecting the concept of *Ihsân* in their interactions with clients (Ibn'Abidin, 1992).

Another core principle is the concept of *Tawhîd*, which emphasises the belief in the oneness of Allāh and the unity of knowledge. Muslim psychologists are expected to integrate this principle into their practice by recognising the spiritual variations across different individuals and considering it for their overall psychological well-being (Rothman & Coyle, 2018). Similarly, upholding the principle of amānah is to bc emphasised. Muslim psychologists must ensure that information shared by clients remain confidential, unless there are legal or ethical obligations to disclose such. They should clearly communicate the limits of confidentiality to clients and obtain informed consent for any necessary disclosures. Upholding the principle of Amanah fosters trust between psychologists and clients, creating a safe and secure therapeutic environment (Sudan, 2017).

The principle of '*adl* (justice) requires Muslim psychologists to treat all clients with fairness and equity, regardless of their cultural or religious background. Practitioners should be knowledgeable about Islāmic teachings and be able to address religious concerns that may arise during therapy with fairness and a clear head. Moreover, the concept of *rahma* (compassion) reminds Muslim psychologists to approach clients with empathy and understanding. This includes being sensitive to the impact of cultural and religious factors on clients' mental health and well-being. Muslim psychologists should engage in ongoing professional development to enhance their cultural competence and ensure that they provide culturally appropriate care to their clients (Rassool, 2014; Zoellner et al., 2021).

Maintaining professional boundaries is also essential for ethical practice. Muslim psychologists should adhere to the guidelines provided by professional organisations, which include maintaining objectivity, avoiding dual relationships and refraining from exploiting their position of power. Islāmic ethics reinforce these guidelines by emphasising the importance of maintaining appropriate boundaries and avoiding situations that could compromise the therapeutic relationship. For example, a Muslim psychologist should avoid engaging in close personal relationships with clients or accepting gifts that could create conflicts of interest. By respecting professional boundaries, psychologists ensure that their focus remains on the well-being of their clients and maintain the integrity of the therapeutic process. In multicultural societies, including those with a significant Muslim population, Muslim psychologists must be aware of and sensitive to cultural and religious differences. They should respect the diversity of clients' backgrounds and beliefs, integrating cultural competence into their practice.

To sum it up, Muslim psychologists face unique ethical considerations due to the intersection of their professional responsibilities and Islāmic principles. One of the main challenges in integrating Islāmic ethics into psychological practice is understanding and working with religious identity. Religious identity holds significant importance in the lives of individuals seeking psychological support. Practitioners must be sensitive to the religious beliefs and practices of their clients, recognising the impact of these factors on their psychological well-being. This necessitates a deep understanding of Islāmic principles and the ability to apply them appropriately in therapeutic settings. By integrating Islāmic ethical guidelines into their practice, Muslim psychologists can provide high-quality care while honouring the values and principles of their faith.

This chapter has highlighted the importance of Islāmic ethical principles, confidentiality, trust, professional boundaries, and addressing cultural sensitivities and religious beliefs. Adhering to these guidelines will enable Muslim psychologists to navigate the complexities of ethical dilemmas and fulfil their professional obligations while upholding their Islāmic values. Ethical considerations in psychotherapy and counselling within an Islāmic context require practitioners to navigate complex dilemmas while upholding Islāmic values and professional standards. Confidentiality, informed consent, and the boundaries of professional relationships are key ethical considerations that practitioners must address. By integrating Islāmic ethical frameworks, practitioners can ensure that their practice aligns with Islāmic principles and promotes the well-being of their clients.

It is important for practitioners to continue engaging in ongoing education and dialogue to deepen their understanding of Islāmic ethics and their application in the field of psychology. Islāmic ethics provides a moral compass for practitioners, guiding them to uphold principles such as justice, beneficence, non-maleficence, and respect for autonomy. However, the multicultural and pluralistic societies of Muslim clients mean practitioners may face additional dilemmas beyond the issue of conflicting secular and Islāmic ethical frameworks. Striking a balance between these cultural nuances and religious edicts can help in such scenarios.

To navigate the ethical challenges in Islāmic psychology, practitioners can draw upon relevant research and case studies. Research can provide insights into the experiences and needs of Muslim clients, offering evidence-based guidelines for ethical practice. For instance, studies have shown that the incorporation of religious and spiritual elements in therapy can have positive effects on the psychological well-being of Muslim clients (Alcorn et al., 2010; Banning et al., 2009). These findings highlight the importance of addressing religious identity ethically and integrating Islāmic principles into therapy. Moreover, case studies can provide practitioners with practical examples of ethical dilemmas and their resolutions in the context of Islāmic psychology. They offer valuable insights into the complexities of working with Muslim clients and the ethical considerations involved. Case studies also serve as learning tools, allowing practitioners to develop their ethical reasoning and decision-making skills in challenging situations.

Various ethical frameworks that can guide practitioners in the field of Islāmic psychology have been examined. These frameworks draw upon Islāmic literature, such as the Qur'ân, the *hādīth*, and the consensus of Islāmic scholars. They provide a foundation for ethical decision-making in psychological practice. For example, the principle of justice in Islāmic ethics emphasises the fair treatment of individuals. In psychotherapy, this principle can be applied by ensuring equal access to services, avoiding discrimination, and promoting cultural competence. The principle of beneficence calls upon practitioners to act in the best interest of their clients and promote their well-being. This can be achieved by providing evidence-based interventions, respecting clients' religious beliefs, and considering the socio-cultural context in therapy.

In addition, the principle of non-maleficence emphasises the avoidance of harm. In psychological practice, this principle can guide practitioners to be mindful of potential negative consequences of their interventions and to prioritise the well-being of their clients. Finally, the principle of respect for autonomy recognises the individual's right to make decisions about their own treatment. Practitioners should respect their clients' autonomy and involve them in the therapeutic process through shared decision-making.

The crux of the discussions so far is that ethical dilemmas are common in the field of psychology, and Islāmic psychology is no exception. If anything, the divergent perspectives of secular and Islāmic ethical frameworks further complicate matters. However, this complication can be handled with cultural competence, religious inclusivity, and investing in therapeutic conduct that prioritises the welfare of the client and their community.

References

Al-Attas, M. N. (1989). *Islām and the philosophy of science*. International Institute of Islāmic Thought and Civilization, International.

Al-Qaradawi, Y. (2013). *The lawful and the prohibited in Islām: الحلال والحرام في الإسلام*. The Other Press.

AbdAllāh Rothman, L. P. C. (2018). An Islāmic theoretical orientation to psychotherapy. *Advance Praise for Islāmically Integrated Psychotherapy, 62*.

Abu Raiya, H., & Pargament, K. I. (2010). Religiously integrated psychotherapy with Muslim clients: From research to practice. *Professional Psychology: Research and Practice*, *41*(2), 181.

Alcorn, S. R., Balboni, M. J., Prigerson, H. G., Reynolds, A., Phelps, A. C., Wright, A. A., Block, S. D., Peteet, J. R., Kachnic, L. A., & Balboni, T. A. (2010). "If God wanted me yesterday, I wouldn't be here today": Religious and spiritual themes in patients' experiences of advanced cancer. *Journal of Palliative Medicine*, *13*(5), 581–588.

Alqahtani, M. M. J., & Altamimi, N. (2016). Code of ethics and professionalism in light of cultural competency: A guideline for Saudi psychologists, supervisors, and trainees. *Psychological Studies*, *61*, 103–112.

American Psychological Association. (2016). *Ethical principles of psychologists and code of conduct*.

Aten, J. D., & Leach, M. M. (2009). *Spirituality and the therapeutic process: A comprehensive resource from intake to termination*. American Psychological Association.

Baasher, T. A. (2001). Islām and mental health. *EMHJ-Eastern Mediterranean Health Journal*, *7*(3), 372–376.

Banning, M., Hafeez, H., Faisal, S., Hassan, M., & Zafar, A. (2009). The impact of culture and sociological and psychological issues on Muslim patients with breast cancer in Pakistan. *Cancer Nursing*, *32*(4), 317–324.

Bhui, K., Warfa, N., Edonya, P., McKenzie, K., & Bhugra, D. (2007). Cultural competence in mental health care: A review of model evaluations. *BMC Health Services Research*, *7*(1), 1–10.

Cucchi, A. (2022). Integrating cognitive behavioural and Islāmic principles in psychology and psychotherapy: A narrative review. *Journal of Religion and Health*, *61*(6), 4849–4870.

Currier, J. M., Fox, J., Vieten, C., Pearce, M., & Oxhandler, H. K. (2023). Enhancing competencies for the ethical integration of religion and spirituality in psychological services. *Psychological Services*, *20*(1), 40.

Dardas, L. A., Bailey Jr, D. E., & Simmons, L. A. (2016). Adolescent depression in the Arab region: A systematic literature review. *Issues in Mental Health Nursing*, *37*(8), 569–585.

Delphin, M. E., & Rowe, M. (2008). Continuing education in cultural competence for community mental health practitioners. *Professional Psychology: Research and Practice*, *39*(2), 182.

Elzamzamy, K., & Keshavarzi, H. (2019). Navigating ethical dilemmas in mental health practice between professional ethics and Islāmic values. *Journal of Islāmic Faith and Practice*, *2*(1), 40–71.

Fares, Z. E. A., Ala'a, B., Gadelrab, H. F., Lin, C.-Y., Aljaberi, M. A., Alhuwailah, A., & Roubi, M. L. (2021). Arabic COVID-19 psychological distress scale: Development and initial validation. *BMJ Open*, *11*(6), e046006.

Hammoud, M. M., White, C. B., & Fetters, M. D. (2005). Opening cultural doors: Providing culturally sensitive healthcare to Arab American and American Muslim patients. *American Journal of Obstetrics and Gynecology*, *193*(4), 1307–1311.

Hanrahan, S. J. (2010). Culturally competent practitioners. In *Routledge handbook of applied sport psychology* (pp. 460–468). Routledge.

Haque, A., Khan, F., Keshavarzi, H., & Rothman, A. E. (2016). Integrating Islāmic traditions in modern psychology: Research trends in last ten years. *Journal of Muslim Mental Health*, *10*(1).

Hashim, R., & Rossidy, I. (2000). Islāmization of knowledge: A comparative analysis of the conceptions of AI-Attas and AI-Fārūqī. *Intellectual Discourse*, *8*(1).

Hasnain, M., Connell, K. J., Menon, U., & Tranmer, P. A. (2011). Patient-centered care for Muslim women: Provider and patient perspectives. *Journal of Women's Health*, *20*(1), 73–83.

Hodge, D. R. (2018). Spiritual competence: What it is, why it is necessary, and how to develop it. *Journal of Ethnic & Cultural Diversity in Social Work*, *27*(2), 124–139.

Ibn'Abidin, M. A. (1992). *Radd al-Muhtar 'ala al-Durr al-Mukhtar*. Bayrut: Dar Al-Fikr.

Kehoe, N. C. (2016). Religious professionals, ethical dilemmas, and mental illness. *Spirituality in Clinical Practice*, *3*(3), 163.

Keshavarzi, H., & Haque, A. (2013). Outlining a psychotherapy model for enhancing Muslim mental health within an Islāmic context. *International Journal for the Psychology of Religion*, *23*(3), 230–249.

Khaleefah, S. (2022). Justice and autonomy in Islāmic bioethics. *Acta Cogitata: An Undergraduate Journal in Philosophy*, *10*(1), 3.

Koenig, H. G., VanderWeele, T., & Peteet, J. R. (2023). *Handbook of religion and health*. Oxford University Press.

Leach, M. M., & Akhurst, J. E. (2023). Informed consent, multiple relationships, and confidentiality: A comparison across four countries. In *Ethics & behavior* (Vol. 33, Issue 3, pp. 231–238). Taylor & Francis.

Malek, M. D. A. (2020). Mental health and social work: The Islāmic perspectives. In *Mental health and social work* (pp. 395–413). Springer.

Mehraki, B., & Gholami, A. (2017). Physical and mental health in Islām. *Middle East Journal of Family Medicine*, *7*(10), 142.

Miller, G. (2003). *Incorporating spirituality in counseling and psychotherapy: Theory and technique*. John Wiley & Sons.

MuhammadTheMerciful. (2023). *Islām and study of human psychology – Shaykh Hamza Yusuf*. YouTube. https://www.youtube.com/watch?v=H-I0bk7r1ew

Pargament, K. I. (2011). *Spiritually integrated psychotherapy: Understanding and addressing the sacred*. Guilford Press.

Plante, T. G. (2007). Integrating spirituality and psychotherapy: Ethical issues and principles to consider. *Journal of Clinical Psychology*, *63*(9), 891–902.

Ramadan, T. (2009). *Radical reform: Islāmic ethics and liberation*. Oxford University Press.

Ramadan, T. (2013). The challenges and future of applied Islāmic ethics discourse: A radical reform? *Theoretical Medicine and Bioethics*, *34*, 105–115.
Rassool, G. H. (2014). *Cultural competence in caring for Muslim patients*. Bloomsbury Publishing.
Rassool, G. H. (2015). *Islāmic counselling: An introduction to theory and practice*. Routledge.
Richards, P. S., & Bergin, A. E. (2004). *Casebook for a spiritual strategy in counseling and psychotherapy*. American Psychological Association.
Rothman, A., & Coyle, A. (2018). Toward a framework for Islāmic psychology and psychotherapy: An Islāmic model of the soul. *Journal of Religion and Health*, *57*, 1731–1744.
Rothman, A., & Coyle, A. (2020). Conceptualizing an Islāmic psychotherapy: A grounded theory study. *Spirituality in Clinical Practice*, *7*(3), 197.
Sabry, W. M., & Vohra, A. (2013). Role of Islām in the management of psychiatric disorders. *Indian Journal of Psychiatry*, *55*(Suppl 2), S205.
Sachedina, A. (2009). *Islāmic biomedical ethics: Principles and application*. OUP USA.
Saged, A. A. G., Mohd Yusoff, M. Y. Z., Abdul Latif, F., Hilmi, S. M., Al-Rahmi, W. M., Al-Samman, A., Alias, N., & Zeki, A. M. (2020). Impact of Qur'ân in treatment of the psychological disorder and spiritual illness. *Journal of Religion and Health*, *59*, 1824–1837.
Siegel, C., Haugland, G., Reid-Rose, L., & Hopper, K. (2011). Components of cultural competence in three mental health programs. *Psychiatric Services*, *62*(6), 626–631.
Smith, T. B., McCullough, M. E., & Poll, J. (2003). Religiousness and depression: Evidence for a main effect and the moderating influence of stressful life events. *Psychological Bulletin*, *129*(4), 614.
Sudan, S. A. (2017). Principles of Islāmic counseling and psychotherapy. *Asian Journal of Management Sciences & Education*, *6*(3), 129–138.
Tanhan, A. (2019). Acceptance and commitment therapy with ecological systems theory: Addressing Muslim mental health issues and wellbeing. *Journal of Positive Psychology and Wellbeing*, *3*(2), 197–219.
Tanios, C. Y., Abou-Saleh, M. T., Karam, A. N., Salamoun, M. M., Mneimneh, Z. N., & Karam, E. G. (2009). The epidemiology of anxiety disorders in the Arab world: A review. *Journal of Anxiety Disorders*, *23*(4), 409–419.
Vieten, C., & Lukoff, D. (2022). Spiritual and religious competencies in psychology. *American Psychologist*, *77*(1), 26.
Wise, E. H., Sturm, C. A., Nutt, R. L., Rodolfa, E., Schaffer, J. B., & Webb, C. (2010). Life-long learning for psychologists: Current status and a vision for the future. *Professional Psychology: Research and Practice*, *41*(4), 288.
Yusuf, H. (2012). *Purification of the heart: Signs, symptoms and cures of the spiritual diseases of the heart*. eBooks2go, Inc.
Zoellner, L. A., Bentley, J. A., Feeny, N. C., Klein, A. B., Dolezal, M. L., Angula, D. A., & Egeh, M. H. (2021). Reaching the unreached: Bridging Islām and science to treat the mental wounds of war. *Frontiers in Psychiatry*, *12*, 599293.

5 Ethical Guidelines for Muslim Psychologists

5.0 Introduction

In the realm of psychological practice, the intersection of faith and professional ethics holds profound significance. As we delve into this chapter, the focus shifts towards ethical guidelines explicitly tailored for Muslim psychologists because of their complex role in psychology practice. For one, in addition to upholding universal ethical principles outlined by organisations like the American Psychological Association (APA), Muslim psychologists are responsible for considering cultural and religious nuances in their practice. For another, Muslim psychologists are taxed with providing mental health services to individuals who seek support while adhering to both the ethical guidelines set by their profession and the Islāmic ethical principles that shape their interactions with their clients (Abu-Raiya & Pargament, 2015). As such, this chapter explores the fundamental Islāmic values that guide Muslim psychologists in their clinical practice, emphasising integrating these principles with professional codes of conduct.

The chapter explores the intricacies of combining Islāmic principles with the responsibilities and challenges inherent in psychology. Recognising the unique considerations that arise when addressing individuals' mental and emotional well-being within the Islāmic framework, this chapter aims to comprehensively understand the ethical imperatives that guide Muslim psychologists in their professional endeavours. The focus is finely tuned to acknowledge and address these unique considerations, emphasising how they impact the process of tending to the mental and emotional well-being of individuals within the Islāmic framework. This chapter seeks to contribute to the ongoing discourse on culturally sensitive and ethically sound psychological practices within the diverse Muslim community by illuminating the nuanced dynamics.

5.1 Islāmic Ethical Principles in Clinical Practice

Muslim psychologists mainly, but not limited to those seeing to the mental health of Muslims, have several basic guidelines that exist across both Islāmic and clinical psychology ethics that they must adhere to.

DOI: 10.4324/9781032658858-7

- **Compassion**

Compassion is a core value emphasised in Islām and serves as a foundation for the therapeutic relationship between Muslim psychologists and their clients (Abu-Raiya & Pargament, 2015). Islāmic teachings emphasise the importance of showing empathy, understanding and care for others, particularly those suffering. Muslim psychologists strive to cultivate compassion by actively listening to their clients, demonstrating empathy, and providing a safe and non-judgemental space for individuals to share their concerns and struggles.

The APA's Ethical Principles of Psychologists and Code of Conduct also recognises the significance of empathy and compassion in therapeutic relationships. The APA code emphasises the psychologist's duty to treat clients with respect, sensitivity and empathy, mirroring the Islāmic value of compassion in clinical practice (Association, 2016).

- **Justice**

Justice is a fundamental Islāmic principle that guides the actions of Muslim psychologists in their clinical practice (Abu-Raiya & Pargament, 2015). Islāmic teachings stress the importance of fairness, equity, and the pursuit of justice in all aspects of life. Muslim psychologists strive to uphold these principles by treating all clients equitably and without discrimination, regardless of their background, ethnicity, or social status.

The APA's Code of Ethics (2016) aligns with this Islāmic value by emphasising the need to provide fair and just services and promoting equal access to psychological services for all individuals. Muslim psychologists integrate this ethical principle into their work, ensuring they adhere to professional standards while upholding Islāmic teachings on justice.

- **Beneficence**

Beneficence, or the act of doing good, is another Islāmic ethical principle that informs the practice of Muslim psychologists (Abu-Raiya & Pargament, 2015). Islāmic teachings emphasise the importance of promoting the well-being of individuals and society. Muslim psychologists integrate this principle into their clinical practice to maximise the benefits and minimise harm for their clients.

The APA's Ethical Principles of Psychologists and Code of Conduct (2016) also highlights the principle of beneficence, emphasising the psychologist's responsibility to contribute to the welfare and well-being of those they serve. Muslim psychologists align with this principle by ensuring that their interventions and treatment plans improve their clients' psychological well-being while considering the cultural and religious dimensions that may be relevant to their clients' lives.

- **Autonomy**

Respect for autonomy is a significant principle in both Islāmic ethics and professional codes of conduct (Abu-Raiya & Pargament, 2015). In Islām, individuals are considered autonomous beings who can make life decisions. Muslim psychologists respect their clients' autonomy by involving them in the decision-making process, providing them with information, and allowing them to make informed choices regarding their treatment.

The APA's Code of Ethics (2016) also emphasises respecting clients' autonomy and promoting their right to self-determination. Muslim psychologists integrate this principle by ensuring that their clients are actively involved in developing treatment goals and plans, empowering them to make decisions that align with their cultural and religious values.

In handling all of these core psychological principles, Muslim psychologists must consciously cultivate a delicate balance between professional ethics and religious-cum-culturally sensitive care. This is because we live in a multicultural and diverse world where it is essential to recognise the importance of culturally sensitive mental health care. Integrating cultural sensitivity allows Muslim psychologists to appropriately address the unique needs of their clients, ensuring their well-being and fostering a sense of trust and mutual understanding in the therapeutic relationship. This way, clients can be confident that their mental health professionals are adhering to the highest standards of ethical practice and considering their cultural and religious context.

Muslim psychologists play a crucial role in this endeavour, seamlessly integrating Islāmic ethical principles into their clinical practice and aligning the principles of compassion, justice, beneficence, and respect for autonomy with the tenets of Islām and the ethical guidelines set by professional organisations like the APA. While Muslims will benefit aplenty from the convergence of Islāmic and professional ethical principles, the intersection creates a framework for ethical and culturally sensitive care that benefits all clients, regardless of their religious or cultural backgrounds (Abu-Raiya & Pargament, 2015). In today's world, where mental health is of paramount importance, the contribution of Muslim psychologists who adhere to both their faith and professional standards is invaluable. This integrated approach offers a model for mental health practitioners of all backgrounds to serve their diverse clientele better, fostering a more inclusive and understanding society.

5.2 The Muslim Psychologist: Uniting Professional and Ethical Principles

As previously noted, Islāmic ethical principles intersect with professional ethics in several domains. This discourse extends further by examining critical areas where divergences in approach may arise within the context of mental health care. It highlights the necessity for Muslim psychologists to navigate these differences thoughtfully, ensuring that the care they provide is both religiously and culturally sensitive. The following sections explore how these considerations manifest across various key aspects of clinical practice.

5.2.1 Confidentiality, Trust, and Professional Boundaries

Confidentiality, trust, and professional boundaries are the cornerstones of effective psychological practice (Corey et al., 1988). In psychology, practitioners across various cultural and religious backgrounds are united by their commitment to these principles. The commitment to confidentiality in the psychology practice among Muslim professionals aligns with ethical standards and finds resonance within the broader Islāmic teachings on trust and respect for privacy. However, Muslim psychologists encounter a distinct set of challenges when reconciling these tenets with the ethical framework of Islām (Iqbal & Skinner, 2021).

Navigating the intersection of confidentiality, trust, and professional boundaries presents a distinctive set of challenges for Muslim psychologists, demanding a delicate balance rooted in Islāmic ethics (Al-Shaar, 2014). While upholding client confidentiality is paramount, these professionals are also responsible for recognising and reporting potential harm, which may sometimes seem at odds with the commitment to secrecy. In Islāmic ethics, there is a strong emphasis on protecting individual privacy, but this must be weighed against situations where harm may befall the client or others. In addition, the establishment of trust is paramount in the therapeutic relationship, but for Muslim psychologists, it is interwoven with religious considerations, such as adhering to Islāmic values and norms. Furthermore, cultural sensitivity becomes a crucial component when delivering psychological care within the context of Islāmic ethics, as it necessitates an understanding of the client's cultural and religious background to foster a therapeutic alliance that is respectful and inclusive.

Hence, for Muslim psychologists, balancing the preservation of confidentiality with the duty to report, for instance, may become an arduous task. In such intricate scenarios where the duty to report potential harm intersects with the principle of confidentiality, Muslim psychologists draw upon the rich tapestry of Islāmic ethics to guide their actions (Ahmed & Amer, 2013). For instance, consider a scenario where a Muslim psychologist is entrusted with information showing that the life of a patient or a close relative is under threat. How should the psychologist act? Islām places a high value on preserving life and the well-being of individuals and communities. The Qur'ân contains numerous verses emphasising the sanctity of life and the importance of promoting well-being. Verses such as Surah Al-Ma'idah (5:32)

"من أجل ذالك كتبنا على بني إسرائيل أنه من قتل نفسا بغير نفس أو فساد في الأرض فكأنما قتل الناس جميعا ومن أحياها فكأنما أحيا الناس جميعا"

- Because of that, We decreed upon the Children of Israel that whoever kills a soul unless for a soul or corruption [done] in the land – it is as if he had slain mankind entirely. And whoever saves one – it is as if he had saved mankind entirely (interpretation of the meaning), likening the value of preserving a single life to saving all humanity.

Islāmic teachings acknowledge the gravity of situations that may pose harm, emphasising the moral imperative (of the Muslim psychologist in this case) to prevent harm and protect others. Muslim psychologists, therefore, approach their professional responsibilities with a nuanced understanding, recognising that the duty to report is not a betrayal of trust but a manifestation of the broader Islāmic principle of prioritising the greater good. In navigating this delicate balance, they are driven by a sense of responsibility to their clients and society, striving to uphold ethical standards while honouring confidentiality as much as possible. This integration of professional guidelines with Islāmic ethics reflects the adaptability of ethical principles to diverse cultural and religious contexts, ensuring that the well-being of individuals and communities remains a paramount concern.

This concept described above is covered under the principle of "*maslaha*". *Maslaha,* rooted in Islāmic jurisprudence, introduces a nuanced perspective to the ethical considerations of confidentiality in psychology (Nyazee, 2019). While the commitment to client privacy is paramount, the concept of "Maslaha" recognises situations where the public interest or the well-being of the individual and community may supersede strict confidentiality (Haddad & Stowasser, 2004). This principle empowers Muslim psychologists to navigate complex ethical dilemmas, especially when disclosure is necessary for the greater good.

In such complex situations, Muslim psychologists may consult with Islāmic scholars or Islāmic ethics committees, seeking a nuanced understanding that aligns with professional standards and religious principles (Ibn Qayyim Al-Jawziyya, 2020). This collaborative approach ensures that decisions align with both professional standards and the ethical teachings of Islam, reflecting a thoughtful and balanced application of confidentiality principles within the context of Islāmic jurisprudence. Engaging with these nuanced ethical considerations also ensures the client's well-being. It reflects the dedication of Muslim psychologists to harmonising their professional responsibilities with the moral imperatives outlined in their faith.

Moreover, the emphasis on trust in the therapeutic relationship goes beyond mere professional standards for Muslim psychologists; it aligns seamlessly with the fundamental principles of Islam (Haque, 2018). A patient must be able to trust that if his psychologist divulges confidential information, it is because it must be disclosed. It will only be divulged to necessary and trustworthy stakeholders. The role of the Muslim psychologist in building and maintaining this trust cannot be overemphasised. As such, even when the psychologist must breach the trust for the greater good, it must be done with absolute kindness and with the patient's emotional health in mind.

The Qur'ân encourages trustworthiness and underscores the importance of compassionate and empathetic interactions. The Prophet Muhammad (ﷺ), considered the exemplar of Islāmic conduct, is quoted as saying, "The believer is not a believer until he trusts, and he does not trust until he loves for his brother what he loves for himself". This profound *hādīth* reinforces the interconnectedness of trust, empathy, and love. In psychology, Muslim practitioners draw inspiration from these teachings, weaving them into the fabric of their therapeutic approach. In addition to upholding confidentiality, Muslim psychologists further enhance the therapeutic relationship by actively integrating Islāmic values and teachings into their practice. This involves respecting the principles of confidentiality outlined in professional standards and incorporating the rich ethical framework provided by Islāmic teachings.

In addition to upholding the principles of trust and client confidentiality, maintaining professional boundaries in psychological practice cannot be overstated. Islāmic ethics is a guiding light for Muslim psychologists navigating these intricacies (Farooqi, 2006). Rooted in the principle of *haya*, or modesty, these ethical guidelines extend beyond personal conduct into the professional sphere. Muslim psychologists are reminded to embody modesty not just in their attire and speech but also in the way they interact with their clients. This emphasis on modest behaviour underscores the importance of creating a safe therapeutic space where individuals can openly explore their concerns without fear of judgement or impropriety (Rogers & Dorfman, 1951).

Essentially, beyond ensuring confidentiality and trust, Muslim psychologists must be steadfast in adhering to the broader spectrum of professional codes of conduct that guide ethical practice in the field. This commitment extends to the prohibition of dual relationships, exploitation, and the maintenance of appropriate boundaries – an ethos shared with their non-Muslim counterparts. Muslim psychologists must recognise the significance of fostering a therapeutic environment where the focus is solely on the well-being of their clients. By prioritising a professional demeanour and steering clear of any potential conflicts of interest, Muslim psychologists underscore their dedication to providing ethical and practical mental health care. This approach not only aligns with universal standards of ethical conduct but also reflects the values inherent in Islāmic teachings, emphasising the importance of integrity and a commitment to the welfare of others.

In addition to upholding confidentiality, Muslim psychologists strongly emphasise cultivating trust through a nuanced integration of Islāmic principles and cultural sensitivity in their therapeutic practice. This culturally informed approach contributes to a deeper understanding of the client's worldview, facilitating more effective communication and rapport. Moreover, Muslim psychologists conscientiously adhere to professional codes of conduct, establishing and maintaining appropriate professional boundaries. This commitment upholds the therapeutic process's integrity, fostering an environment where clients feel secure in sharing their thoughts, emotions, and concerns.

The amalgamation of ethical standards, professional boundaries, and a dedication to building trust underscores the holistic and inclusive nature of ethical practice among Muslim psychologists. In seamlessly weaving Islāmic ethics into their practice, Muslim psychologists go beyond the conventional boundaries of psychological care, creating a harmonious intersection of faith and professional competence. This integration upholds the principles of confidentiality and extends to encompass a broader spectrum of cultural sensitivity and inclusivity.

5.2.2 Addressing Cultural Sensitivities and Religious Beliefs

In addition to upholding confidentiality and trust, Muslim psychologists actively strive to provide culturally sensitive and inclusive care by weaving cultural and religious considerations into the therapeutic journey. However, this requires that these psychologists recognise that even where Islām unites them, Muslim patients have varying cultural backgrounds and world views. Recognising and embracing cultural diversity goes beyond mere tolerance for Muslim patients; it is an integral aspect of Muslim psychologists' approach to providing effective psychological care (Ali & Awaad, 2019). These professionals understand that each client's cultural background contributes to their unique identity and influences how they perceive and navigate the world. Still, the challenge that Muslim psychologists face lies in striking a delicate balance between adhering to professional standards and recognising the significance of intrareligious and intercultural nuances.

Navigating the intersection of multiculturalism and psychology requires Muslim psychologists to blend ethical considerations with cultural sensitivity skilfully. As they engage with clients from diverse cultural backgrounds and varying religious beliefs, psychologists must embrace the principles of inclusivity and respect. Incorporating Islāmic principles into therapy becomes an art, as psychologists draw on the teachings of the Qur'ân to foster understanding and empathy. This harmonious integration enhances the therapeutic alliance and reflects the psychologist's commitment to providing inclusive and respectful mental health care in multicultural societies.

By integrating the teachings of Islam, Muslim psychologists not only acknowledge the importance of cultural sensitivity but also actively incorporate it into their therapeutic strategies (Ahmed & Amer, 2013). The following Qur'ânic verse, serves as a guiding principle, encouraging psychologists to foster an environment where clients feel heard and understood, irrespective of cultural differences.

.وجعلناكم شعوبا وقبائل لتعارفوا

- and made you peoples and tribes that you may know one another.

(Qurān 49:13)

This commitment to cultural sensitivity enriches the therapeutic relationship and aligns with the broader Islāmic ethos of fostering harmony and mutual respect among diverse communities. In doing so, Muslim psychologists contribute to the broader goal of promoting mental health and well-being within the context of cultural competence and understanding. Understanding the diverse nature of the Muslim community, these psychologists acknowledge the importance of tailoring their approach to each individual's unique cultural and religious nuances. This may manifest in accommodating prayer times during therapy sessions or integrating Islāmic teachings that resonate with the client's concerns.

These practices are classified under the umbrella principle of *cultural competence*. Cultural competence is a fundamental principle in psychology that promotes understanding, respecting, and valuing diverse cultures and belief systems. Muslim psychologists must strive to develop cultural competence to engage with clients from different backgrounds effectively. This includes gaining knowledge about Islāmic practices, customs, and values and recognising the diversity within the Muslim community. This commitment to cultural competence goes beyond a mere acknowledgement of religious practices; it extends to a deep understanding of the nuances and intricacies within the diverse Muslim communities.

Muslim psychologists recognise their clients' vast diversity in cultural backgrounds, traditions, and belief systems, as Islām encompasses a rich tapestry of cultural practices from various regions. To be truly effective in their practice, these psychologists learn about the cultural contexts that shape their clients' experiences. This involves staying informed about Islam's various schools of thought, understanding the impact of cultural influences on individual perspectives, and remaining open to continuous learning.

Self-awareness is also crucial for Muslim psychologists, who must acknowledge their own cultural biases, stereotypes, and assumptions that could influence their interactions with clients. Reflecting on personal values and biases allows psychologists to provide unbiased and non-judgemental care. To provide culturally sensitive care, Muslim psychologists must avoid making assumptions based on stereotypes or biases. They should approach each client with an open mind and treat them as individuals rather than as representatives of a particular culture or religion. Recognising the uniqueness of each client's experience is essential in fostering a therapeutic alliance based on trust and respect. Culturally sensitive care in psychology demands a nuanced understanding that transcends stereotypes and biases. Muslim psychologists play a crucial role in dismantling preconceived notions, ensuring that they approach each client as a unique individual rather than a mere reflection of their cultural or religious background.

In handling clients' religious beliefs, Muslim psychologists must be mindful of the fact that religious beliefs and practices often play significant roles in the lives, attitudes, and belief systems of Muslim patients. Psychologists must, therefore, carefully integrate religious principles into therapy when appropriate and desired by the client. However, it is crucial to respect clients' autonomy and not impose religious beliefs or practices on them. In addition, where clients seek to exclude their religious beliefs from their therapeutic encounters, Muslim psychologists must respect this decision. Recognising the profound impact of religious beliefs on the lives of Muslim clients, it becomes imperative for Muslim psychologists to navigate the delicate balance between incorporating religious principles into therapy and respecting individual autonomy.

While understanding and acknowledging the importance of religious practices, psychologists must approach this integration with sensitivity and openness. Creating a space where clients feel comfortable expressing their spiritual concerns can enhance the therapeutic process, fostering a deeper connection between the psychologist and the client. Psychologists need to be tuned to the client's preferences, only integrating religious elements into therapy at the exact moments when it aligns with the client's wishes. This approach ensures that the therapeutic journey remains client-centred, honouring each individual's faith's diverse and personal nature while upholding the principles of respect and autonomy.

Integrating religious beliefs into therapy involves a nuanced approach beyond mere acknowledgement, striving for a deeper understanding of the client's faith journey. Psychologists may employ strategies such as exploring the client's unique interpretation of their faith, exploring how it shapes their perspectives, and examining the impact on their thoughts and behaviours. In addition, incorporating religious rituals or teachings that resonate with the client's belief system can be a powerful tool in promoting psychological well-being. The overarching goal is to empower individuals to reconcile their religious values with their growth objectives, fostering a holistic approach to mental health that recognises and respects the intricate interplay between faith and psychological well-being.

When Muslim psychologists encounter ethical dilemmas or uncertainty regarding religious matters, they should seek guidance from Islāmic scholars. Islāmic scholars are well-versed in Islāmic jurisprudence and can provide insights into how Islāmic principles and ethics can be applied in therapeutic contexts. Seeking guidance from Islāmic scholars enhances Muslim psychologists' ethical foundation and ensures that their practice aligns harmoniously with religious principles. These scholars, equipped with profound knowledge of Islāmic jurisprudence, serve as valuable resources for navigating complex ethical dilemmas that may arise in psychology. Their insights contribute to a more nuanced understanding of how Islāmic values can seamlessly integrate into therapeutic practices.

Consultation with Islāmic scholars can help psychologists navigate complex issues related to religious beliefs, cultural norms, and ethical considerations. This collaboration between psychology and religious scholarship bolsters Muslim psychologists' professional development and fosters a comprehensive approach to ethical decision-making. The synergy between psychological expertise and religious guidance also enriches the quality of care provided to clients within a framework that respects professional standards and religious convictions. The collaboration ensures that the therapeutic interventions align with Islāmic values and do not inadvertently contradict religious teachings. Engaging in consultation with Islāmic scholars adds an invaluable layer of depth to the ethical framework within which psychologists operate.

In handling religious and culturally sensitive issues, Muslim psychologists should adhere to ethical guidelines and professional codes of conduct relevant to their field. These guidelines, such as those provided by the APA or other professional organisations, serve as frameworks for ethical decision-making and promote clients' well-being. While general ethical principles apply universally, Muslim psychologists can refer to specific cultural and religious consideration guidelines. These guidelines also underscore that embracing a culturally sensitive approach is crucial for fostering a deep understanding of clients' backgrounds and values. Muslim psychologists may find further guidance in specific ethical guidelines that cater to the intersection of psychology and Islam. For example, Malik (2020) offers advice on ethical issues unique to Muslim psychologists, including confidentiality, informed consent, and cultural sensitivity.

Here are a few key considerations to summarise the discussions in this section. Addressing cultural sensitivities and religious beliefs is an essential aspect of ethical practice for Muslim psychologists. Second, integrating religious beliefs into therapy and respecting client autonomy can enhance treatment outcomes. Also, seeking guidance from Islāmic scholars and adhering to relevant ethical guidelines and professional codes of conduct ensure ethical and culturally sensitive care. Furthermore, incorporating cultural sensitivity and religious awareness into therapeutic practices contributes to ethical guidelines and enriches the overall quality of mental health care. All these considered, Muslim psychologists, in their commitment to understanding and respecting diverse cultural backgrounds, must recognise the significance of tailoring therapeutic approaches to align with the unique needs of their clients. This approach extends beyond merely avoiding stereotypes; it involves actively understanding the cultural and religious contexts that shape individuals' worldviews.

5.3 Practicing Psychology from the Islāmic-cum-Ethical Viewpoint

In psychology, ethical guidelines serve as a framework to ensure clients' and practitioners' well-being and integrity. For Muslim psychologists, incorporating Islāmic ethical principles into their practice further strengthens their commitment to providing holistic care that aligns with their religious values. Islām emphasises the ethical dimensions of human behaviour and encourages individuals to cultivate virtues such as honesty, compassion, and justice. These principles can be applied to the therapeutic relationship guiding Muslim psychologists in client interactions. Incorporating Islāmic teachings reinforces the importance of honesty, compassion, and justice within the therapeutic space.

Drawing from the rich ethical tapestry of Islām, psychologists can navigate complex situations with a profound understanding of the human experience. For instance, the Qur'ânic emphasis on empathy and compassion resonates in the therapeutic approach, fostering an environment where clients feel genuinely understood and supported. In essence, the integration of Islāmic ethics goes beyond mere adherence to professional standards; it becomes a pathway to providing a more comprehensive, culturally sensitive, and spiritually aligned form of mental health care. This approach benefits Muslim clients seeking therapy and contributes to the broader dialogue on the intersectionality of faith and psychological well-being.

The integration of Islāmic ethical principles into the practice of Muslim psychologists is of paramount importance. The ethical guidelines provided by professional organisations, such as the APA, further support Muslim psychologists in adhering to the ethical standards of their profession. As the field of psychology continues to evolve, the integration of Islāmic ethics will continue to play a crucial role in ensuring the well-being and spiritual growth of Muslim clients while empowering Muslim psychologists to uphold the highest standards of professional conduct. The seamless integration of Islāmic ethical principles into the practice of Muslim psychologists not only enhances the quality of care provided but also reinforces the harmonious coexistence of religious values and professional standards.

Muslim psychologists create a therapeutic environment that resonates with their client's cultural and religious sensitivities by weaving both Islāmic and professional perspectives and ethical principles like confidentiality, trust, and professional boundaries into the fabric of their practice. This integration is not a divergence from established professional guidelines but rather a nuanced approach that enriches the field by acknowledging diverse cultural and religious contexts. As the landscape of psychology continues to evolve, the incorporation of Islāmic ethics serves as a beacon, guiding practitioners to navigate the complexities of individual well-being while maintaining the utmost integrity and respect for diverse belief systems. In this way, the integration of Islāmic ethical principles becomes not just a practice but a cornerstone for fostering a holistic and inclusive approach to mental health care.

References

Abu-Raiya, H., & Pargament, K. I. (2015). Religious coping among diverse religions: Commonalities and divergences. *Psychology of Religion and Spirituality*, *7*(1), 24.

Ahmed, S., & Amer, M. M. (2013). *Counseling Muslims: Handbook of mental health issues and interventions*. Routledge.

Ali, S., & Awaad, R. (2019). Islamophobia and public mental health: Lessons learned from community engagement projects. In *Islamophobia and psychiatry: Recognition, prevention, and treatment* (pp. 375–390). Springer.

Al-Shaar, N. (2014). *Ethics in Islam: Friendship in the political thought of al-Tawhidi and his contemporaries*. Routledge.

American Psychological Association. (2016). *Ethical principles of psychologists and code of conduct*.

Corey, G., Corey, M. S., & Callanan, P. (1988). *Issues and ethics in the helping professions*. Wadsworth/Thomson Learning.

Farooqi, Y. N. (2006). Understanding Islāmic perspective of mental health and psychotherapy. *Journal of Psychology in Africa*, *16*(1), 101–111.

Haddad, Y. Y., & Stowasser, B. F. (2004). *Islāmic law and the challenges of modernity*. Rowman Altamira.

Haque, A. (2018). Psychology from an Islāmic perspective. In *Global psychologies: Mental health and the global south* (pp. 137–150).

Ibn Qayyim Al-Jawziyya, I. Q. (2020). *Ranks of the divine seekers: A parallel English-Arabic text. Volume 1* (Vol. 14). Brill.

Iqbal, N., & Skinner, R. (2021). Islāmic psychology: Emergence and current challenges. *Archive for the Psychology of Religion*, *43*(1), 65–77.

Malik, R. (2020). *Islāmic ethics and psychology*. Center for Islāmic Legislation and Ethics. https://www.cilecenter.org/resources/articles-essays/Islāmic -ethics-and-psychology

Nyazee, I. A. K. (2019). *Islāmic jurisprudence*. Lulu. com.

Rogers, C. R., & Dorfman, E. (1951). *Client-centered: Its current practice, implications, and theory*. ICON Group International.

Part III

Contemporary Issues in Islāmic Ethics and Psychology

6 Islāmic Ethics and Social Justice

6.0 Introduction

The concept of social justice is deeply ingrained in the Islāmic tradition and serves as a guiding principle for addressing contemporary issues in ethics and psychology. Within the rich tapestry of Islāmic teachings, the concept of social justice emerges as a cornerstone that reflects the ethical underpinnings of the faith and provides a blueprint for navigating the complex landscape of contemporary challenges in ethics and psychology. In this chapter, we will explore Islāmic perspectives on social justice, drawing upon relevant Islāmic texts, scholarly works, and social justice frameworks to illuminate the nuanced and multifaceted ways in which Islām not only endorses but actively champions the principles that underlie a just and harmonious society. By navigating the intersections of theology, ethics, and psychology, this exploration seeks to unravel the intricacies of how Islāmic teachings can contribute meaningfully to contemporary discussions on fostering a more equitable and compassionate world.

6.1 Social Justice in the Islāmic Tradition

Islām's emphasis on fairness extends beyond mere rhetoric, underscoring the imperative of creating a just society where everyone is treated equitably and compassionately. Social justice is a central theme in the Islāmic tradition, rooted in the Qur'ân, the *hādīth,* and the scholarly works of Muslim theologians throughout history (Al-Ghazālī, 2015; Ibn Kathir, 2000). The Qur'ân and *Hādīth*, the foundational texts of Islām, resonate with directives that champion the cause of the marginalised, advocate for the rights of the oppressed, and prescribe a collective responsibility to alleviate societal injustices. The Qur'ân, the primary source of guidance for Muslims, contains numerous verses highlighting the significance of justice (Ibn Kathir, 2000).

For example, in Surah Al-Nisai (4:135), the Qur'ân states:

يأيها الذين ءامنوا كونوا قوامين بالقسط شهداء لله ولو على أنفسكم أو الوالدين والأقربين

DOI: 10.4324/9781032658858-9

- O you who have believed, be persistently standing firm in justice, witnesses for Allah, even if it be against yourselves or parents and relatives.

This verse emphasises the Muslim's obligation to uphold justice even in challenging circumstances, without bias or favouritism. The Qur'ân's profound emphasis on justice extends beyond mere rhetoric, embedding within it a profound philosophy that transcends personal inclinations or affiliations. It fosters a holistic understanding of justice that necessitates unwavering commitment, urging believers to stand firm and bear witness for the sake of Allah, even if it means going against one's interests or those of loved ones. This call to impartiality underscores the universality of justice, portraying it as an essential virtue that transcends familial, societal, or personal boundaries. By stressing the importance of justice comprehensively, the Qur'ân promotes a society founded on equity and fairness, where individuals are encouraged to navigate moral dilemmas with an unwavering commitment to what is right. In essence, these verses from Surah Al-Nisai dictate a code of conduct for individual believers and lay the foundation for a just and harmonious society where righteousness prevails over self-interest.

Scholars throughout Islāmic history have further developed the concept of social justice within the Islāmic framework. They have explored the multifaceted dimensions of justice and its applications in various spheres of life. Scholars of Islāmic jurisprudence, ethics, and psychology alike have drawn from the Qur'ân and *Hādīth* to make significant contributions to the understanding and application of social justice within the Islāmic framework. One notable scholar, Imam Al-Ghazālī, emphasised the connection between individual piety and social justice (Al-Ghazālī, 2015). He argued that personal righteousness and ethical conduct are inseparable from the pursuit of justice and the well-being of society. Imam Al-Ghazālī's profound insights into the relationship between individual righteousness and social justice continue to resonate throughout Islāmic history, shaping the discourse on ethical conduct and societal well-being. His teachings underscore the interconnectedness of personal virtue and the broader pursuit of justice, portraying them as symbiotic elements crucial for fostering a harmonious society.

Al-Ghazālī's emphasis on the ethical dimension of justice goes beyond mere legalistic interpretations, encouraging believers to internalise a sense of moral responsibility in their daily lives. In his perspective, true justice extends beyond formal institutions and laws, reaching into the hearts and actions of individuals. This holistic approach to social justice has inspired subsequent scholars to delve deeper into the ethical underpinnings of Islāmic teachings, fostering a tradition where personal righteousness becomes a catalyst for positive change in the collective well-being of society. Through the centuries, these intellectual explorations have contributed to the rich tapestry of Islāmic thought on social justice, reinforcing that ethical conduct is a personal duty and a fundamental building block for a just and compassionate community.

In the contemporary context, scholars have drawn upon the rich Islāmic ethical tradition to address social justice issues. For instance, Islāmic psychologists have explored the intersection of social justice and psychology from an Islāmic perspective (Ahmed & Amer, 2013). Their work highlighted the need to address social inequalities and systemic oppression to ensure individuals' and communities' well-being and psychological health. Exploring the intersection between social justice and psychology within the Islāmic context represents a crucial step towards recognising and addressing the intricate links between systemic inequalities and psychological well-being. By shedding light on the impact of social disparities, her work contributes to the field of Islāmic psychology and underscores the imperative of incorporating justice into broader societal frameworks.

Aside from Islāmic psychology scholars, many contemporary Islāmic scholars have also engaged with social justice frameworks to provide Islāmic perspectives on issues such as poverty, economic inequality, and human rights. Ramadan (2001) is one of such prominent Islāmic scholars. He has emphasised the importance of justice and equality in the economic sphere, advocating for ethical, economic practices that prioritise the well-being of all members of society. These scholars' endeavours reflect a broader movement within the realm of Islāmic thought to integrate principles of social justice into various facets of life. These scholars extend social justice discourse into the economic realm, emphasising the ethical dimensions of economic practices. In particular, Ramadan's advocacy for justice and equality in economic matters reflects a commitment to creating societies where economic systems prioritise the welfare of all individuals, transcending traditional boundaries and aligning with the principles of social justice within the Islāmic ethical framework.

Beyond the works of individual scholars, Islāmic centres have not been left out of the endeavours aimed at defining the scope of social justice in Islām and upholding social justice in society. One such influential centre is the Research Centre for Islāmic Legislation and Ethics (CILE), which combines Islāmic principles with psychological insights to analyse and address contemporary challenges. Established in 2012, CILE is a dedicated institution specialising in Islāmic legislation and ethical thought, with a distinctive emphasis on applied ethics. Rooted in a vision of reform and renewal, CILE draws inspiration from the fundamental principles of the Holy Qur'ân, the *Sunnah*, and the higher objectives of Islām. Nestled within the Faculty of Islāmic Studies, Hamad Bin Khalifa University in Doha, Qatar, CILE serves as a beacon of scholarship and dialogue, embodying a commitment to advancing ethical solutions grounded in Islāmic principles for the contemporary challenges faced by societies worldwide. CILE is the leading institute dedicated to the intersection of Islāmic ethics, psychology, and social justice.

The centre endeavours to furnish a robust methodological and theoretical framework that transcends the realm of academia, aspiring to contribute to practical applications that effect transformative change in the world, fostering justice and ethics. By enabling collaboration between scholars steeped in textual knowledge and those attuned to contextual realities, CILE seeks to engage in discourse on the day's critical issues. In alignment with its mission, CILE extends its reach to diverse global audiences, encompassing experts, activists, practitioners, students, and ordinary individuals who share common concerns and interests.

Among the Qur'ân, *Hādīth*, Islāmic centres, Islāmic researchers, and Islāmic psychology practitioners, significant contributions have been made to scholarly discourse on social justice, offering valuable insights for both Muslim and non-Muslim communities seeking to foster just and equitable societies. Furthermore, the commitment to social justice demonstrated in the Qur'ân, *Hādīth*, and works of prominent Islāmic-cum-Islāmic psychology scholars shapes the ethical framework that guides Muslims in their daily lives. Below are a few well-known applications of social justice within the Islāmic tradition.

6.1.1 Social Justice, Irrespective of Race, and Tribe

Islāmic teachings emphasise the importance of justice and equality for all individuals, regardless of their social status, gender, or background. The principles of social justice in Islām are firmly grounded in the belief that all human beings are equal before God and deserve fair treatment in all aspects of life. The Qur'ân repeatedly calls for justice and fairness, emphasising the need to uphold the rights of individuals and promote equality. For example, in Surah Al-Hujurat (49:13), the Qur'ân states:

"يأيها الناس إنا خلقناكم من ذكر وأنثى وجعلناكم شعوبا وقبائل لتعارفو إن أكرمكم عند الله أتقاكم إن الله عليم خبير"

- O mankind, indeed We have created you from male and female and made you peoples and tribes that you may know one another. Indeed, the most noble of you in the sight of Allah is the most righteous of you. Indeed, Allah is Knowing and Acquainted. (interpretation of the meaning)

This verse highlights the Islāmic belief in all human beings' equal worth and dignity, regardless of race, gender, or social status. The verse exemplifies this emphasis on equality, urging humanity to recognise the diversity inherent in their creation. The verse emphasises that the varied origins of individuals, spanning different genders, ethnicities, and tribes, are a deliberate design fostering mutual understanding. In asserting that the noblest in the eyes of Allāh is the most righteous, the Qur'ân transcends superficial markers of identity, encouraging believers to prioritise moral integrity over external characteristics. This profound recognition of human equality establishes a foundation for a just society, promoting a worldview that acknowledges every individual's inherent worth and dignity, echoing principles that resonate across diverse cultural and religious landscapes. In essence, the Qur'ân's teachings on ethics lay the groundwork for a compassionate and equitable social order that regards all humans as equal regardless of their colour, physical attributes, or origins.

6.1.2 Social Justice in Interpersonal Interactions

The Qur'ân repeatedly underscores the imperative of upholding justice, encouraging believers to be compassionate, fair, and empathetic in their interactions with others. Moreover, the Prophet Muhammad (ﷺ) exemplified justice and compassion in his interactions with others, and his teachings provide valuable insights into the Islāmic understanding of social justice. In one famous *Hādīth*, the Prophet Muhammad (ﷺ) said, "None of you truly believes until he loves for his brother what he loves for himself" (Sunan Ibn Majah 66). This statement emphasises the importance of empathy and solidarity, urging Muslims to treat others fairly and equally. The ethical teachings found in this *Hādīth* are not merely historical anecdotes but enduring lessons that continue to shape Islāmic ethics.

The *Hādīth* encapsulates the essence of Islāmic ethics, underlining the fundamental importance of empathy and solidarity. This statement transcends its temporal origin, resonating as a timeless directive calling Muslims to cultivate a spirit of fairness, equality, and benevolence in their relationships with others. Through this particular *Hādīth* and many others in the *Hādīth* literature, believers gain profound insights into the Prophet's exemplary life, which serves as a guiding light for navigating the complexities of contemporary social justice issues within the framework of Islāmic ethics.

6.1.3 Social Justice as a Collective Responsibility

Islāmic ethics strongly emphasises the concept of "amr bil ma'ruf wa nahy anil munkar", which translates to "enjoining good and forbidding evil". This principle encourages Muslims to promote justice and actively confront injustice in society. It is not enough for individuals to avoid engaging in unjust actions; they are also obligated to work towards rectifying societal injustices. Islāmic ethics, rooted in amr bil ma'ruf wa nahy anil munkar principles, extends beyond individual conduct to advocate for collective responsibility in fostering a just society. This concept underscores the proactive role that Muslims are called to play in addressing and remedying societal imbalances. It reinforces the idea that abstaining from wrongdoing is only one facet of ethical behaviour; equally important is the imperative to collectively and actively promote righteousness and oppose injustice.

This ethos propels Muslims to engage with the world around them, fostering an environment of equity and compassion. The notion of enjoining good and forbidding evil transcends the personal sphere, highlighting the interconnectedness of individuals within the broader community. In practising this ethical guideline, Muslims are not merely passive observers but dynamic participants in the ongoing struggle for justice and moral rectitude, striving to create a society that reflects the principles of compassion, fairness, and virtue. These interventions address individual psychological well-being and target systemic issues, aiming to dismantle oppressive structures and promote social justice. The synergy of Islāmic ethics with psychological practice thus catalyses transformative change, fostering empowerment among marginalised individuals and contributing to the broader mission of creating a more equitable and compassionate society.

6.1.4 Economic Justice as a Catalyst for Social Equity

Within the rich tapestry of the Islāmic tradition, economic justice is intricately woven into the very fabric of societal principles. Islām advocates for individual spiritual development and underscores the community's collective responsibility to address economic disparities. Economic justice is a fundamental social justice aspect within the Islāmic tradition (El-Ashker & Wilson, 2006). Islām promotes an economic system that seeks to alleviate poverty, ensure fair distribution of wealth, and prevent exploitation. For instance, the concept of *zakāt*, one of the Five Pillars of Islām, epitomises this commitment to economic justice by requiring the well-off to contribute a proportion of their wealth to those in need. This concept (*zakāt*, better explained in Chapter 2) aims to redistribute wealth within the society, from the affluent to the less fortunate, to ensure social justice. This mandatory charitable contribution becomes a powerful mechanism for fostering a sense of equality, solidarity, and empathy within the Muslim community.

In addition, Islāmic finance principles promote ethical banking practices prioritising social welfare. This financial framework emphasises fairness, transparency, and social welfare, steering away from exploitative practices such as usury (a practice known to aid the rich at the expense of the poor). In essence, the Islāmic economic system strives to create a harmonious society where economic prosperity is shared equitably, reinforcing that social justice is not merely a lofty ideal but an integral part of the Islāmic ethos.

6.1.5 Gender Equality in the Islāmic Tradition of Social Justice

Gender justice is another critical dimension of social justice in Islām. Islāmic teachings emphasise the equitable treatment of men and women, recognising their equal worth and dignity. While cultural practices in some Muslim-majority societies may deviate from these principles, the Qur'ânic teachings stress the importance of gender equity. For example, in Surah Al-Ahzab (33:35), the Qur'ân states:

"إن المسلمين والمسلمات والمؤمنين والمؤمنات والقانتين والقانتات والصادقين
والصادقات والصابرين والصابرات والخاشعين والخاشعات والمتصدقين
والمتصدقات والصائمين والصائمات والحافظين فروجهم والحافظات والذاكرين
الله كثيرا والذاكرات أعد الله مغفرة وأجرا عظيما"

Indeed, the Muslim men and Muslim women, the believing men and believing women, the obedient men and obedient women, the truthful men and truthful women, the patient men and patient women, the humble men and humble women, the charitable men and charitable women, the fasting men and fasting women, and the men who guard their private parts and the women who do so – for them, Allah has prepared forgiveness and a great reward.

Gender justice within the framework of Islām extends beyond the mere acknowledgement of equality between men and women; it delves into the nuanced aspects of their respective roles, responsibilities, and rights. The verse from Surah Al-Ahzab underscores the equal worth and dignity of men and women and delineates various qualities and virtues expected of both genders. This inclusivity in listing characteristics signifies that righteousness knows no gender, and both men and women are called upon to embody qualities such as truthfulness, patience, humility, and charity. Islām emphasises the shared spiritual journey of men and women, recognising that their devotion, piety, and ethical conduct contribute equally to the well-being of the community and society.

While interpretations and applications of gender justice may vary across Muslim communities, the essence of Islāmic teachings encourages a harmonious coexistence where both men and women complement each other in fulfilling their roles and responsibilities, fostering a society built on principles of justice and equity. Furthermore, Islām places a strong emphasis on the rights of marginalised communities, including orphans, widows, and people with low incomes. The Prophet Muhammad (ﷺ) himself was known for advocating for the rights of the vulnerable and oppressed among women and children. His teachings and actions serve as a guiding light for Muslims seeking to establish social justice and alleviate the suffering of marginalised individuals.

6.2 The Islāmic Perspective on Human Rights and Equality

Islām, as a comprehensive religious and social system, offers a unique perspective on human rights and equality. It emphasises the inherent dignity and worth of every human being, grounded in the belief that God creates all individuals and possesses intrinsic rights and responsibilities. This perspective is derived from the Qur'ân, the central religious text of Islām, and the teachings of the Prophet Muhammad (ﷺ). This Islāmic perspective on human rights and equality extends beyond mere theological doctrine; it encompasses a practical framework for fostering justice and compassion in the socio-political sphere. The Islāmic perspective on social justice is also relevant to contemporary debates on human rights. As a religion recognising every individual's inherent dignity and rights, Islām promotes a comprehensive framework encompassing civil, political, economic, and social rights.

Islām emphasises equality before the law, irrespective of social status, race, or ethnicity. The Qur'ân underscores the notion that all humans are equal members of the broader human family, discouraging discrimination and prejudice. Numerous verses of the Qur'ân also affirm the sanctity of human life and the importance of justice and fairness. For instance, Surah Al-Ma'idah (5:32) states:

". . .من قتل نفسا بغير نفس أو فساد في الأرض فكأنما قتل الناس جميعا ومن أحياها فكأنما أحيا الناس جميعا. . ."

that whoever kills a soul unless for a soul or corruption [done] in the land – it is as if he had slain mankind entirely. And whoever saves one – it is as if he had saved mankind entirely.

This verse underscores the sanctity of human life and the prohibition of unjust killing. It forms the basis for the Islāmic prohibition of violence and promoting peaceful coexistence.

The profound message encapsulated in Surah Al-Ma'idah (5:32) of the Qur'ân goes beyond emphasising the sanctity of human life; it also establishes a profound ethical framework for the Islāmic perspective on justice, peace, and coexistence. This verse goes beyond the condemnation of unjust killing; it presents a holistic philosophy that highlights the interconnectedness of humanity. The analogy drawn between the killing of one soul and the destruction of all of mankind serves as a poignant reminder of the collective responsibility to protect and preserve life. Islāmic teachings, rooted in this and similar verses, promote a society where individuals are not only discouraged from causing harm but are encouraged to contribute to the well-being of others actively. This perspective not only forms the basis for the prohibition of violence within the Islāmic tradition but also underscores the imperative of fostering a world characterised by compassion, justice, and mutual respect. In embracing the teachings of Surah Al-Ma'idah, Muslims are called to champion the value of human life, thereby contributing to creating a harmonious and just social order.

Islām also emphasises the concept of equality before God. Qur'ân (49:13) states:

"يأيها الناس إنا خلقناكم من ذكر وأنثى وجعلناكم شعوبا وقبائل لتعارفو إن أكرمكم عند الله أتقاكم. . ."

> O mankind, indeed We have created you from male and female and made you peoples and tribes that you may know one another. Indeed, the most noble of you in the sight of Allah is the most righteous of you.

This verse from Surah Al-Hujurat highlights that the worth and superiority of individuals are not based on their ethnicity, race, or social status but on their piety and righteousness. This profound verse from the Qur'ân encapsulates the essence of Islāmic teachings on equality by underlining the fundamental principle that all human beings share a common origin and purpose. By acknowledging the diversity of humans, the Qur'ân encourages people to embrace this diversity to understand one another.

It underscores that the intrinsic value of an individual is not determined by external factors such as nationality, race, or social standing but rather by the purity of their heart and the righteousness of their actions. In essence, Islām promotes a universal brotherhood where individuals are judged by the content of their character and their devotion to moral and ethical principles. This emphasis on spiritual merit over superficial distinctions fosters an inclusive and harmonious society, reinforcing that genuine nobility lies in one's commitment to goodness and virtue, transcending the boundaries of worldly classifications.

Furthermore, the teachings of Prophet Muhammad (ﷺ) serve as a guiding light, illustrating through his actions the importance of treating everyone fairly and kindly. Practical examples abound from the Prophet Muhammad's (ﷺ) life, showcasing his dedication to justice, especially in his dealings with marginalised and vulnerable members of society. The profound impact of these teachings is evident in the rich history of Islāmic civilisations, where scholars and rulers alike sought to implement policies that promoted inclusivity, addressed socio-economic disparities, and upheld fundamental human rights. The *Hādīth* literature also provides valuable insights into the Prophet Muhammad's (ﷺ) teachings on social justice. The Prophet Muhammad (ﷺ) is reported to have said, "Help your brother, whether he is an oppressor or he is oppressed".

When asked how to help an oppressor, the Prophet (ﷺ) responded, "By stopping him from oppressing others". This *Hādīth* highlights the Islāmic principle of intervening to prevent injustice and promote human rights to establish a just society. This profound *Hādīth* encapsulates the essence of empathy and compassion and underscores the Islāmic commitment to fostering social harmony and equity. By urging believers to assist both the oppressed and the oppressor, the Prophet Muhammad (ﷺ) elucidates a holistic approach to justice that transcends mere partisanship. The subsequent guidance to curb the oppressor's actions emphasises the proactive role that individuals should play in upholding justice, reinforcing the idea that upholding human rights begins with the ability to stop injustice. Essentially, it is not sufficient to be passive observers of wrongdoing. Instead, Islām encourages a collective responsibility to intervene and rectify social imbalances, contributing to establishing a society built on the principles of fairness, equality, and compassion. This *Hādīth* and many more like it promotes a vision of social justice that extends beyond retribution, advocating for transforming oppressive dynamics into a collective pursuit of a just and harmonious community.

Islām envisions a society where justice prevails, the weak are protected, and the powerful are held accountable. In embracing this comprehensive human rights approach, Islām offers a moral and ethical foundation for individual conduct and provides a blueprint for creating harmonious and just communities. The interplay between spiritual values and societal principles within Islām fosters a holistic understanding of human rights deeply rooted in compassion, fairness, and the recognition of the inherent dignity of every person. Today, the call for social justice remains a dynamic force within Muslim communities, inspiring individuals to advocate for the rights of the oppressed, challenge systemic inequalities, and work towards fostering a society that reflects the compassionate and egalitarian ideals embedded in Islāmic teachings.

The Islāmic concept of *Ummah* further contributes to understanding human rights and equality. The Ummah refers to the global Muslim community, transcending national, racial, and ethnic boundaries. This concept fosters a sense of solidarity, empathy, and mutual responsibility among Muslims. Qur'ân (21:92) states:

"إن هذه أمتكم أمة واحدة وأنا ربكم فاعبدون"

Indeed this, your religion, is one religion, and I am your Lord, so worship Me.

The concept of Ummah proposed in this verse of Surah Al-Anbiya encourages Muslims to stand united in their worship of God, uphold justice, promote human rights, and address social inequalities. The Islāmic concept of "Ummah" thus serves as a robust framework that goes beyond the religious sphere, extending into social justice and human rights. The idea of a global Muslim community emphasises the interconnectedness of humanity, promoting a collective responsibility toward justice and equality.

By transcending national, racial, and ethnic boundaries, the concept of "Ummah" encourages Muslims to recognise the shared humanity that binds them together. This transcendent perspective is reinforced by the Qur'ânic verse that underscores the oneness of the Muslim community, highlighting a divine call to worship and serve the common good. Consequently, the concept of Ummah acts as a catalyst for Muslims to actively address societal disparities, advocate for human rights, and foster a sense of empathy and solidarity beyond the confines of individual identity or geographical location. Essentially, the Ummah drives positive social change grounded in justice and compassion.

Scholars of Islāmic ethics and psychology have extensively discussed the compatibility of Islāmic teachings with contemporary human rights frameworks. They argue that the Qur'ân and the *Hādīth* provide a solid foundation for human rights advocacy. However, they also acknowledge that interpretations and applications of Islāmic teachings can vary, leading to diverse perspectives on human rights within Muslim-majority societies (Abdullah, 2014; Ansari, 2012; Haque et al., 2016; Seedat, 2020). These diverse perspectives and interpretations of Qur'ânic verses on social justice are believed to be due to the richness and depth of Islāmic jurisprudence and the dynamic evolution of societal norms across diverse Muslim nationalities.

Consequently, within Muslim-majority societies, the discourse on human rights is multifaceted, reflecting a range of perspectives that intersect with cultural, historical, and political contexts. This is why contemporary scholars such as Tariq Ramadan, Abdullahi An-Na'im, and Khaled Abou El Fadl emphasise the need for contextualised interpretations of Islāmic principles and an engagement with international human rights standards (An-Na'im, 2000; Hunter et al., 2005; Ramadan, 2009). Their emphasis on contextualised interpretations of Islāmic principles and alignment with international human rights standards underscores a nuanced approach to bridging the gap between religious values and universal rights. They argue that Islāmic ethics and human rights can be mutually reinforced, as both aim to protect individuals' dignity, freedom, and well-being. They further assert that social justice frameworks can complement Islāmic teachings in promoting human rights and equality. As such, in exploring the intricate discourse surrounding the intersection of Islāmic principles with contemporary human rights, scholars have not only scrutinised the Qur'ân and the *Hādīth* for their inherent support of human rights but have also underscored the nuanced nature of interpretations within the diverse Muslim community.

Writers like Asma Barlas and Ziba Mir-Hosseini have also explored the intersection of feminism, gender equality, and Islāmic ethics. They advocate for the reinterpretation of Islāmic texts and critically analyse patriarchal interpretations that may undermine gender equality (Barlas, 2019; Mir-Hosseini, 2006). These scholars highlight the importance of justice and equity in dismantling discriminatory practices and promoting inclusive societies. Their advocacy for a reinterpretation of Islāmic texts and a critical analysis of patriarchal interpretations demonstrates a commitment to dismantling gender-based discrimination within Islāmic frameworks. By championing justice and equity, these scholars aim to address and rectify historical biases perpetuating gender inequality. Their work underscores the transformative potential of integrating social justice frameworks into Islāmic teachings, fostering inclusive societies that honour human rights and equality principles.

In addition to the works of these scholars, the Cairo Declaration on Human Rights in Islām, ratified and adopted by member states of the Organisation of Islāmic Cooperation, equally presents an Islāmic perspective on human rights that is consistent with Islāmic teachings and values. As a pivotal document in discussions of human rights in the modern political sphere, the Cairo

Declaration serves as a testament to Islām's comprehensive approach to social justice and a holistic framework spanning civil, political, economic, and social dimensions. Crafted in alignment with Islāmic teachings and values, the declaration not only articulates the rights and responsibilities of individuals but also emphasises the interconnectedness of these rights with broader societal welfare. In doing so, it underscores the compatibility of Islāmic principles with the universal pursuit of justice and human dignity, offering a unique lens through which to navigate the intricate terrain of human rights in our contemporary global landscape.

To sum up this section, we must reiterate that Islām's perspective on human rights and equality is rooted in the Qur'ân and the teachings of Prophet Muhammad (ﷺ). Islām emphasises the inherent dignity of every human being, equality before God, and the concept of "Ummah" as a means of fostering solidarity and cooperation. Islām also underscores the concept of *zakāt*, or obligatory charity, as a means to address systemic injustice and structural inequalities. Furthermore, scholars and thinkers alike have engaged in discussions about the compatibility of Islāmic teachings with human rights frameworks, highlighting the importance of contextual interpretations and engaging with international standards. Social justice frameworks and feminist perspectives have also contributed to advancing human rights and equality within the Islāmic ethical framework. Ultimately, these discussions and ongoing efforts aim to promote a just and equitable society based on a perspective that harmonises the principles of Islām with the broader notions of universal human rights, ensuring a balanced and inclusive approach to societal development.

6.3 Addressing Injustice and Oppression in Psychological Practice

This discussion of social justice will be incomplete without a glance at the pervasive issues of injustice and oppression that Islāmic psychologists come across in addressing mental health issues afflicting individuals and communities (Smith, 2015). This section explores the practical implications of addressing these challenges from an Islāmic perspective, drawing upon Islāmic texts, scholarly works, and social justice frameworks (Abou El Fadl, 2014; Ramadan, 2009). The goal is to provide Islāmic psychologists with clear guidelines from the Islāmic perspective on social justice, giving valuable insights they can borrow from to confront and alleviate the profound impacts of injustice and oppression on the mental health of their patients. By integrating Islāmic ethics into psychological interventions, professionals can help foster healing and transformative change in individuals with mental health challenges, and in communities where social injustices are perpetuated.

A more nuanced approach emerges when viewed through the lens of the Islāmic perspective, where the amalgamation of spiritual principles and social justice becomes a guiding force for psychology practitioners. Rooted in Islāmic texts and scholarly insights, this approach acknowledges the existence of societal inequalities and seeks to redress them through therapeutic strategies that echo the teachings of compassion, fairness, and empathy found in Islām. The approach proposes that practitioners can transcend conventional therapeutic boundaries by infusing Islāmic ethics into psychological interventions to create a more holistic and culturally sensitive framework.

Integrating Islāmic ethical and social justice interventions into psychology practice enables professionals to facilitate individual healing and a broader societal transformation. Through a synergistic blend of psychological expertise and Islāmic values, practitioners stand poised to empower individuals and communities, catalysing a ripple effect of positive change that extends far beyond the confines of the therapeutic setting. Particularly, practitioners can look to Islāmic ethics, which encompasses a rich array of values that can guide psychologists in addressing injustice and oppression (Al-Ghazzali, 2010). Compassion (*rahmah*), mercy (*rahma*), equity (*'adālah*), and fairness (*'adl*) are fundamental principles emphasised in Islāmic ethics.

Incorporating these values into therapeutic approaches can facilitate a compassionate and empathetic therapeutic alliance, allowing individuals to feel understood, validated, and supported in their experiences of injustice (Smith, 2015). The Qur'ân states:

"وما أرسلناك إلا رحمة للعالمين"

"And We have not sent you, [O Muúammad], except as a mercy to the worlds" (Qur'ân 21:107), highlighting the prophetic role in exemplifying mercy and compassion. But being merciful to fellow human beings is not the sole responsibility of the Prophet Muhammad (ﷺ); psychology practitioners must also exemplify these foundational Islāmic ethical principles-mercy and compassion-as a first step towards promoting social justice. Islāmic teachings emphasise the responsibility of every individual to stand against oppression and injustice, urging believers to advocate for fairness and equity in their communities. The therapeutic process thus becomes a microcosm of the more significant societal endeavour to foster compassion and address systemic issues. This holistic approach recognises the interconnectedness of personal well-being and social harmony, underscoring the potential of Islāmic principles to inform and enrich the practice of psychology in the pursuit of a more just and compassionate world.

Professionals can adopt a strengths-based approach focusing on resilience, agency, and empowerment (Abu Raiya & Pargament, 2010). Addressing injustice and oppression requires a deep understanding of the unique experiences and challenges faced by diverse Muslim populations. For one, psychologists must be fair, must believe in the equality of all races and ethnicities, and must acknowledge their Muslim patients from all walks of life as worthy individuals. By acknowledging every individual's inherent dignity and worth, psychological interventions can help individuals reframe their experiences of oppression, fostering a sense of agency and empowerment. This strengths-based approach underscores the importance of fostering resilience and empowerment as integral components of psychological interventions. The approach aligns with the Islāmic belief in the intrinsic worth of every human being as created by Allah, as stated in Qur'ân (17:70):

ولقد كرمنا بني آدام

We have certainly honoured the children of Adam.

Furthermore, it is essential for psychologists to be culturally sensitive and knowledgeable about the cultural, social, and historical contexts that shape their clients' experiences (Smith, 2015). Islām is a diverse and global religion, encompassing various ethnicities, languages, and cultural practices. Therefore, professionals should engage in ongoing education and training to enhance their cultural competency and develop a nuanced understanding of the complexities of Muslim identities, even as more identities continue to evolve (Whaley, 2008). To effectively implement the principles of a strengths-based approach, professionals must explore a comprehensive understanding of the cultural nuances embedded within diverse Muslim populations. By cultivating cultural sensitivity and staying informed about the historical and social contexts shaping these experiences, psychologists can tailor their interventions to better serve the needs of their Muslim clients. In doing so, they contribute to creating a therapeutic environment that not only recognises but actively honours the rich tapestry of Muslim identities, fostering a sense of agency and empowerment among individuals grappling with oppression.

Scholarly works and social justice frameworks can provide valuable insights in this regard. Contemporary scholars, such as Khaled Abou El Fadl and the aforementioned Tariq Ramadan, have contributed extensively to the field of Islāmic ethics and social justice (Abou El Fadl, 2014; Ramadan, 2009). Their works explore the intersections of Islām, social justice, and psychology, shedding light on the multifaceted dimensions of addressing injustice and oppression within Muslim communities. Furthermore, contemporary frameworks such as critical race theory and intersectionality offer valuable lenses through which to examine the complex dynamics of power, privilege, and oppression (Crenshaw, 1989; Delgado & Stefancic, 2023). By incorporating these frameworks into psychology practice, professionals can gain a deeper understanding of the intersecting identities and experiences of individuals affected by injustice and oppression. They can also enhance their capacity to contribute meaningfully to the ongoing discourse on social justice within diverse communities.

By infusing these principles into therapeutic spaces, mental health professionals can foster environments that not only acknowledge the pain caused by injustice but also empower individuals and communities to navigate the path towards healing and resilience. The importance of ongoing education and cultural competency cannot be overstated, particularly when working with diverse Muslim populations, as it ensures that practitioners are equipped with the nuanced understanding required to address the unique challenges faced by each individual. Furthermore, the utilisation of Islāmic texts and scholarly works, coupled with an awareness of broader social justice frameworks, offers a robust foundation for psychology practitioners to contribute meaningfully to the promotion of healing and transformative change in the lives of those adversely affected by injustice and oppression. Through this holistic and informed approach, professionals can play a pivotal role in fostering psychological well-being and social equity within Muslim communities and beyond.

References

Abdullah, F. (2014). Virtues and character development in Islāmic ethics and positive psychology. *International Journal of Education and Social Science*, *1*(2), 69–77.

Abou El Fadl, K. (2014). *Reasoning with god: Reclaiming Shari 'ah in the modern age*. Rowman & Littlefield.

Abu Raiya, H., & Pargament, K. I. (2010). Religiously integrated psychotherapy with Muslim clients: From research to practice. *Professional Psychology: Research and Practice*, *41*(2), 181.

Ahmed, S., & Amer, M. M. (Eds.). (2013). *Counseling Muslims: Handbook of mental health issues and interventions*. Routledge.

Al-Ghazālī, A. H. (2015). *Ihya"ulum al-din: The revival of the religious sciences*. Islāmic Book Trust.

Al-Ghazzali. (2010). *The alchemy of happiness*. Cosimo Classics. https://books.google.com.ng/books?id=htx2zqa0TNkC

An-Na'im, A. A. (2000). Islām and human rights: Beyond the universality debate. *Proceedings of the ASIL Annual Meeting*, *94*, 95–101.

Ansari, Z. (2012). Islāmic psychology. In *Religious theories of personality and psychotherapy* (pp. 325–357). Routledge.

Barlas, A. (2019) *Believing women in Islam: Unreading patriarchal interpretations of the Qur'an*. University of Texas Press.

Crenshaw, K. (1989). Demarginalizing the intersection of race and sex: A black feminist critique of antidiscrimination doctrine, feminist theory and antiracist politics. *University of Chicago Legal Forum*, *1989*(1), 139.

Delgado, R., & Stefancic, J. (2023). *Critical race theory: An introduction* (Vol. 87). NYU Press.

El-Ashker, A., & Wilson, R. (2006). *Islāmic economics: A short history* (Vol. 3). Brill.

Haque, A., Khan, F., Keshavarzi, H., & Rothman, A. E. (2016). Integrating Islāmic traditions in modern psychology: Research trends in last ten years. *Journal of Muslim Mental Health*, *10*(1).

Hunter, S. T., Malik, H., Mayer, A. E., Abou El Fadl, K., Hassan, R., Ibrahim, S. E., & Pastor, R. A. (2005). *Islām and human rights: Advancing a U.S.-Muslim dialogue. Religion and human rights*. http://doi.org/10.1017/S2044251311000166

Ibn Kathir, I. (2000). Tafsîr ibn kathîr. Dar-Us-Salam.

Mir-Hosseini, Z. (2006) 'Muslim women's quest for equality: Between Islamic law and feminism', *Critical inquiry, 32*(4), 629–645.

Ramadan, T. (2001). *Islam, the West and the challenges of modernity*. The Islāmic Foundation.

Ramadan, T. (2009). *Radical reform: Islāmic ethics and liberation*. Oxford University Press.

Seedat, M. (2020). Signifying Islāmic psychology as a paradigm: A decolonial move. *European Psychologist, 26*(2), 131–141.

Smith, L. (2015). *Psychology, poverty, and the end of social exclusion: Putting our practice to work*. Teachers College Press.

Whaley, A. L. (2008). Cultural sensitivity and cultural competence: Toward clarity of definitions in cross-cultural counselling and psychotherapy. *Counselling Psychology Quarterly, 21*(3), 215–222.

7 Ethical Foundations of Islāmic Research on Humans

7.0 Introduction

Research within the realm of Islāmic studies necessitates a thoughtful exploration of ethical considerations that align with the principles and values inherent in Islāmic teachings. This chapter delves into the ethical dimensions researchers must navigate when conducting studies related to Islāmic psychology. With a focus on methodological considerations, the ethics of human subjects research within the Islāmic context, and the imperative need to address bias and cultural appropriation, this chapter aims to provide a comprehensive framework for scholars and practitioners engaging in Islāmic research. By spotlighting the Islāmic ethical perspectives on human subject research, this chapter fosters a deeper understanding and appreciation of the diverse dimensions of the Islāmic worldview.

This chapter explores methodological considerations in Islāmic psychology research, recognising the unique blend of spiritual, cultural, and psychological factors that shape the Islāmic worldview. Researchers are challenged to adopt methodologies that respect and integrate these dimensions, ensuring a holistic and culturally sensitive approach to studying psychological phenomena within the Islāmic context. The discussion turns to the ethics of human subjects research in an Islāmic context. Drawing upon the principles of Islāmic jurisprudence and ethical guidelines, this section addresses informed consent, confidentiality, and protecting participants' rights.

Recognising the potential pitfalls of misrepresentation and misunderstanding, the section also provides insights into fostering cultural competence among researchers and mitigating biases that may influence the research process. By promoting a more nuanced and respectful approach, this chapter aims to contribute to the establishment of ethical standards in Islāmic research. As we explore ethical considerations in Islāmic research, we hope that researchers, scholars, and practitioners will find guidance in navigating the complexities of conducting studies within the rich tapestry of Islāmic thought and culture. Through a conscientious approach to methodology, human subjects' ethics, and the avoidance of bias, researchers, scholars, and practitioners can contribute to elevating ethical standards in Islāmic research.

DOI: 10.4324/9781032658858-10

7.1 Methodological Considerations in Islāmic Psychology Research

The term "research" in Arabic generally conveys the idea of "seeking out" or "investigating" something. It is also called al-Tahqiq, signifying inquiry, exploration, or examination. From an Islāmic perspective, research extends beyond merely acquiring knowledge; it is a comprehensive concept that integrates theory, practice, and education, all deeply rooted in moral and sociopolitical contexts. The research process typically functions within a defined theoretical framework, known as the research paradigm, which is shaped by underlying philosophical perspectives. For Muslim researchers, this framework is grounded in a worldview shaped by values and principles derived from the Qur'ân, the *Sunnah*, and the rich legacy of Islāmic civilisation (Rassool, 2023, 2024).

In conducting research within an Islāmic framework, it is crucial to leverage methodological foundations that align with Islāmic principles. For instance, Islāmic approaches to research in psychotherapy involve integrating Islāmic principles, values, and perspectives into the research process. These approaches aim to align research methodologies with the ethical and spiritual foundations of Islām. Key aspects of such methodologies include adherence to the Islāmic worldview, Islāmic ethics, incorporation of the spiritual dimension, interdisciplinary perspectives, engagement with Islāmic scholars, community-based research, validation of Islāmic interventions, and longitudinal studies.

Research in Islāmic psychotherapy significantly benefits from employing mixed-methods approaches instead of relying exclusively on a single methodology. By integrating qualitative and quantitative research methods, scholars can better understand therapeutic interventions' effectiveness and cultural relevance. A newly developed research approach in Islāmic scholarship, grounded in the Islāmic worldview, adopts a systematic methodology that emphasises connectivity, holism, and emergence as its core principles. Unlike traditional research methods that primarily focus on identifying and analysing a problem statement, the maqasid methodology prioritises defining the purpose of the research. It incorporates iterative cycles of reflection on the Qur'ân and *Sunnah* alongside critical analysis of existing literature, real-world contexts, framework development, and the formulation of theories and principles. This methodology is structured into five distinct steps, from establishing a clear purpose to formulating conclusive theories and principles, emphasising engaging with the Qur'ân, and integrating its teachings into the research process (Rassool, 2023, 2024).

Islāmic psychology research, for example, seeks to integrate Islāmic beliefs, values, and practices into studying human behaviour and mental processes. Several guidelines and methodologies have been proposed to ensure the integrity and ethicality of such research while acknowledging the unique ethical considerations entrenched in various Islāmic frameworks. These guidelines go beyond conventional methodologies, aiming to seamlessly weave Islāmic beliefs, values, and practices into the fabric of understanding human behaviour and mental processes.

These considerations encompass a commitment to respect human dignity, ensure informed consent, and adhere to principles of justice, mirroring the broader ethical ideals enshrined in Islāmic teachings. This integration is not merely a superficial overlay but a conscious effort to delve into the essence of Islāmic teachings and their implications on the psyche. Through the conscientious application of these methodologies, Islāmic psychology research strives to contribute to academic discourse and enrich the understanding of human psychology in a way that aligns with the spiritual and ethical dimensions of Islāmic tradition.

Researchers must, therefore, navigate the delicate balance of incorporating Islāmic values into their methodologies while maintaining scientific rigour. By adopting systematic approaches such as the maqasid methodology and integrating insights from the Qur'ân and *Sunnah*, research within the Islāmic framework can achieve its ultimate aim: to advance knowledge in a manner that aligns with divine guidance and ethical integrity. The following methodological considerations are essential in any Islāmic psychology research.

7.1.1 Islāmic Epistemology

One key methodological consideration is the integration of Islāmic epistemology into the research process. Islāmic epistemology emphasises the importance of knowledge derived from both revelations (the Qur'ân and *Hādīth*) and empirical observation (Ali & Al-Owaihan, 2008). Researchers are encouraged to draw upon both sources of knowledge, thereby adopting a holistic approach that acknowledges the spiritual dimensions of human behaviour and psychological well-being. This approach fosters a nuanced comprehension of human behaviour and psychological well-being, recognising that individuals are not solely products of their observable experiences but are also influenced by unseen forces. In adopting such a holistic perspective, researchers embark on a journey that transcends conventional methodologies, opening avenues for a more profound exploration of the intricate interconnections between faith, human cognition, and societal dynamics.

Integrating Islāmic epistemology into psychology research enriches the research landscape, allowing for a more inclusive and culturally sensitive examination that resonates with the lived experiences of individuals within Islāmic societies. Incorporating Islāmic epistemology into the research process adds depth and cultural sensitivity to the investigation and aligns the study with a comprehensive understanding of the world. By embracing the dual pillars of revelation and empirical observation, researchers create a framework that respects the interplay between the spiritual and the empirical realms.

7.1.2 Ethical and Moral Considerations

In addition to epistemology, Islāmic ethics and moral values are two critical methodological considerations in Islāmic psychology research design and implementation (Abū-Rabia, 2013; Dasti et al., 2020). Islāmic ethics, within the realm of Islāmic psychology research, provides a comprehensive framework for addressing ethical dilemmas often faced by psychology researchers, especially regarding preserving the well-being and dignity of research participants. Therefore, following Islāmic ethics in Islāmic psychology research means employing methodologies that align with Islāmic values and ethical guidelines.

These include ensuring informed consent, maintaining confidentiality, and respecting the dignity and well-being of research participants. It also means researchers must uphold principles such as justice, fairness, beneficence, and non-maleficence in all stages of the research process (Abū-Raiya & Pargament, 2015). Within the purview of these principles, ensuring the well-being and dignity of research participants becomes a paramount objective, underscoring the responsibility researchers bear in producing quality research and upholding Islāmic ethical frameworks.

7.1.3 Cultural Sensitivity and Inclusivity

Islāmic psychology researchers must strive for cultural sensitivity and inclusivity. This involves recognising and respecting the diversity of Muslim populations worldwide and incorporating their cultural norms, values, and practices into the research design (Lee et al., 2017). Researchers should be mindful of potential biases and strive to avoid cultural appropriation by consulting with relevant community members and experts. The ethical considerations extend beyond universal principles, encompassing cultural sensitivity and inclusivity. Recognising the global rich tapestry of Muslim populations, researchers must conscientiously integrate diverse cultural norms, values, and practices into the research design. Achieving these demands more than a surface-level acknowledgement, it necessitates a genuine commitment to understanding and respecting the intricacies of various communities.

Researchers are challenged to sidestep potential biases and avoid cultural appropriation by actively engaging with relevant community members and consulting experts. Furthermore, exploring the rich tapestry of Islāmic traditions and practices is essential to grasp the multifaceted dimensions of human behaviour and mental processes. This holistic approach enhances the credibility of Islāmic psychology research and contributes to establishing ethical practices that honour the cultural diversity inherent in the Muslim world. One crucial aspect of this involves acknowledging the diversity within the Muslim community, recognising the various interpretations of Islāmic teachings, and accommodating these variations in the research framework.

Researchers should also consider the gender and cultural norms within Islāmic societies to ensure the inclusivity and appropriateness of their research methods. In the realm of Islāmic psychology research, the commitment to aligning methodologies with Islāmic values and ethical principles underscores a profound understanding of the cultural and religious context in which studies are conducted. Beyond the procedural aspects of obtaining informed consent, safeguarding confidentiality, and prioritising the welfare of participants, researchers are called upon to delicately navigate the gender dynamics and cultural norms inherent in Islāmic societies. This demands a nuanced approach that acknowledges and respects the diversity within these communities, ensuring that research methods are inclusive and culturally sensitive.

7.1.4 ***Data Collection Methods***

In Islāmic psychology research, the importance of culturally sensitive data collection methods cannot be overstated. Data collection methods in Islāmic psychology research should be sensitive to cultural and religious factors. Researchers must consider the diverse socio-cultural backgrounds of participants and ensure that data collection instruments are culturally appropriate and valid within an Islāmic context. Recognising the diverse socio-cultural backgrounds of participants is paramount, as it allows researchers to tailor their approaches to be both respectful and relevant within the Islāmic context.

The challenge lies in creating an environment where participants feel comfortable expressing themselves authentically while adhering to the cultural and religious frameworks that shape their worldview. Consequently, a meticulous integration of cultural considerations into the research process enhances the validity of findings. It fosters a more inclusive and respectful approach to understanding the complexities of psychological phenomena within the Islāmic context. Cultural sensitivity is crucial when designing instruments such as self-report questionnaires and interview protocols. These tools should not only be linguistically accurate but also attuned to the intricacies of Islāmic norms and values.

In addition to traditional psychological research methods, researchers may also consider incorporating methods such as content analysis of religious texts, observation of religious practices, and engagement with religious scholars and community leaders to gain insights into the psychological experiences of individuals within the Islāmic framework (Abū Raiya & Pargament, 2010). These methods can provide valuable data that goes beyond conventional psychological research approaches. Content analysis of religious texts offers an insightful lens into the core principles and teachings that shape individuals' cognitive and emotional landscapes within the Islāmic faith. Examining the nuances and interpretations embedded in these sacred texts can unveil unique psychological patterns and contribute to a more nuanced comprehension of how religious beliefs influence mental well-being.

Furthermore, observing various religious practices allows researchers to witness the embodied expressions of spirituality first-hand, unravelling the intricate interplay between rituals and psychological states. Engaging with religious scholars and community leaders complements these methods by providing a qualitative depth to the exploration, offering personal narratives, providing cultural contexts, and contextualising the intricate relationships between religious identity and psychological well-being.

7.1.5 Data Analysis

In the realm of Islāmic psychology research, scholars must navigate the intricacies of data analysis with a profound awareness of the distinctive interpretative frameworks embedded in Islāmic teachings. Traditional Western-centric methodologies might not suffice in capturing the multidimensional interplay between psychological phenomena and Islāmic beliefs and practices. As such, when analysing data in Islāmic psychology research, researchers must carefully explore the unique interpretative frameworks that Islāmic teachings offer (Iqbal & Skinner, 2021). Analysis techniques should be adapted to capture the multidimensional nature of psychological phenomena about religious beliefs and practices.

Researchers may consider employing mixed method approaches that combine qualitative and quantitative analysis to provide a more comprehensive understanding of psychological processes within the Islāmic context. This amalgamation can offer a more holistic and nuanced understanding of the intricate psychological processes at play within the tapestry of Islāmic thought, facilitating accurate interpretation and the development of interventions and strategies that are culturally resonant and contextually relevant.

It is equally crucial for researchers to interpret their findings while considering the cultural and religious nuances that may influence the meaning and implications of the results (Ali, 1988)This ensures that the research's conclusions are accurate, valid, and relevant to the specific context of Islāmic psychology. To incorporate cultural and religious nuances into scientific inquiry, researchers must first navigate the complex landscape of cultural and religious diversity, developing a keen understanding of how various cultural and religious perspectives define the psychological experiences of diverse research subjects. This is particularly essential in disciplines such as Islāmic psychology, where the intricate interplay between culture and religion significantly shapes individuals' perceptions and behaviours.

An important benefit Islāmic psychology researchers stand to gain from factoring in the religious, cultural, and contextual intricacies embedded in their study population is that it enhances the validity of their research. It also contributes to the broader goal of fostering inclusivity in the scientific discourse. Moreover, it promotes a nuanced comprehension of psychological phenomena, acknowledging the diversity of human experiences and how each experience is vastly different by the slightest variations in cultural and religious norms.

From the foregoing, several things are precise. Islāmic psychology research necessitates methodological considerations that integrate Islāmic epistemology, ontological perspectives, and conceptual frameworks (Abū-Raiya & Pargament, 2015). To this end, scholars must engage in a nuanced approach that harmonises traditional scientific methodologies with the rich tapestry of Islāmic thought. In delving into the realm of Islāmic psychology research, researchers must balance scientific rigour and the incorporation of Islāmic principles to produce valid and culturally sensitive research outcomes. Striking this balance is paramount, ensuring that the scientific rigour of the research is upheld while concurrently honouring the unique worldview and values enshrined in Islāmic teachings.

To do this, researchers must fundamentally understand the epistemological and ontological underpinnings intrinsic to Islāmic teachings, as this forms the bedrock upon which research inquiries are built. Researchers must equally embark on a delicate journey, navigating the intersections of empirical investigation and incorporating Islāmic principles, thereby fostering a holistic comprehension of psychological phenomena within an Islāmic context. This integration extends beyond theoretical considerations, requiring the formulation of culturally sensitive conceptual frameworks that resonate with the lived experiences of individuals within Islāmic communities.

To traverse this intellectual terrain ethically, researchers must conscientiously adhere to established ethical guidelines, employing methodologies that reflect both the universal standards of scientific inquiry and the ethical tenets specific to Islāmic research practices. Drawing on a comprehensive understanding of Islāmic research ethics and research ethics, researchers thereby contribute to advancing knowledge in Islāmic psychology and fostering mutual understanding and appreciation across diverse religious and cultural landscapes.

7.2 Ethics of Human Subjects Research in an Islāmic Context

Islāmic ethics strongly emphasise the protection of human rights and the dignity of individuals. Therefore, conducting research on human subjects in an Islāmic context requires adherence to a set of ethical guidelines (Lombardi, 2005). These guidelines are rooted in Islāmic principles and provide a framework for ensuring the protection, well-being, dignity, and autonomy of research participants. The ethical guidelines crafted for such research within the Islāmic context are deeply entrenched in the principles derived from Islāmic teachings. These principles include autonomy, beneficence, and non-maleficence.

7.2.1 *Autonomy and Preservation of Participants' Rights*

Central to the Islāmic ethical guidelines for researching human subjects is the imperative to prioritise the well-being and autonomy of research participants. The principle of autonomy, known as *al-hurriyyah* in Arabic, recognises an individual's right to make informed decisions regarding their participation in research. The commitment to protecting research participants' rights underscores profound respect for the sanctity of human life. It emphasises the ethical responsibility of researchers to conduct studies that advance knowledge and preserve the integrity and dignity of each individual involved. Autonomy, therefore, emphasises the need for researchers to respect this right by providing research subjects with all the information necessary to make informed decisions and secure informed consent. Researchers must obtain informed consent from participants, ensuring they clearly understand the research objectives, procedures, potential risks, and benefits.

7.2.2 *Informed Consent*

Beyond participant autonomy, informed consent forms an essential principle in Islāmic research ethics. Furthermore, informed consent facilitates complete autonomy. It involves providing clear and comprehensive information about the research's purpose, procedures, risks, benefits, and potential outcomes while ensuring participants' understanding and autonomy in decision-making. In addition to this, Islāmic research ethics further emphasises the need to consider participants' cultural and religious backgrounds and their level of understanding when providing information to secure informed consent. This is essential as participants, even when Muslims come from varying sociocultural backgrounds that influence their daily choices and their psychology. Consent becomes equally critical where there is potential for data sharing or publication, requiring researchers to seek participants' permission explicitly. Researchers must thus obtain voluntary and informed consent from participants before their inclusion in a study and before the study outcomes are shared or published.

7.2.3 *Fairness Towards Research Subjects*

In addition to the foundational principle of informed consent, Islāmic research ethics also emphasises the ethical treatment of participants throughout the research process. This extends beyond the initial consent phase and involves a continuous commitment to safeguarding the well-being and dignity of participants. Researchers are ethically obliged to uphold the principles of justice, fairness, and respect, ensuring that the potential benefits of the research are distributed equitably.

7.2.4 Justice and Compassion

Islāmic ethics, rooted in the principles of justice and compassion, profoundly emphasise respecting and safeguarding human dignity in all facets of life. Islāmic research ethics further underscores the ethical responsibility of researchers to conduct their studies with a sense of moral integrity, reflecting a broader commitment to the well-being of individuals and the community. The principle of justice, or *al-'adl*, requires the equitable, fair, and unbiased treatment of research participants. Researchers must ensure fair selection criteria for participation, equal access to research opportunities, and clear of any form of discrimination or exploitation. This includes conducting their research without favouring specific individuals or groups based on considerations of gender, age, socio-economic status, race, and other similar factors. By adopting this principle of *'adl*, researchers can ensure inclusivity and fairness in the research process. Furthermore, the principle of justice underscores the fair distribution of research burdens and benefits, aligning with Islāmic teachings of equity and fairness. Researchers must equally be vigilant in minimising any potential harm or discomfort that participants may experience during the study.

7.2.5 Privacy and Confidentiality

Privacy and confidentiality are also of utmost importance in Islāmic research ethics. Researchers are mandated to take necessary measures to protect the privacy and confidentiality of participants' personal information. This includes storing data securely, anonymising data when possible, and obtaining participants' permission for data sharing or publication. Important as this is, in the realm of Islāmic research ethics, the commitment to privacy and confidentiality extends beyond the mere protection of participants' personal information. It encompasses a profound respect for the individual's right to maintain the sanctity of their identity and experiences. Thus, researchers are tasked with securing data storage, anonymising information and fostering an environment of trust and discretionary use of sensitive information.

Thus, confidentiality in Islāmic research ethics upholds the trust between researchers and participants and safeguards their dignity. In upholding the principles of justice and confidentiality in Islāmic research ethics, researchers are not only tasked with the fair selection of participants but also with the responsible management of the information gathered during the research process. Together, both (i.e. justice and confidentiality) underscore the profound trust placed in researchers by participants who share their experiences, ensuring that sensitive information remains shielded from unauthorised access and participants are treated fairly. This commitment to confidentiality serves as a legal requirement and a moral obligation rooted in the Islāmic value system. By prioritising safeguarding personal details and research data, Islāmic research ethics seeks to fortify the bond of trust between researchers and participants, fostering an environment where individuals feel secure in contributing to the advancement of knowledge without fear of compromise or exploitation.

7.2.6 Beneficence

Islāmic research ethics encourages research that promotes human well-being, addresses societal issues, and contributes to the development of Islāmic knowledge and understanding, and this is the crux of Beneficence as a research principle. Beneficence, or *al-ihsan*, guided by the Islāmic ethos of promoting goodness and preventing harm to individuals and society, highlights the researcher's obligation to maximise benefits and minimise harm. Beneficence requires researchers to act in the best interests of the participants and society as a whole. It necessitates a proactive approach where researchers strive to design studies that advance academic knowledge and have tangible implications for improving human well-being and resolving societal challenges.

For example, researchers must ensure that their studies have the potential to generate knowledge that benefits individuals, communities, or society at large, be it as a contribution that improves religious practice, mental health or daily livelihood. Consequently, beneficence underscores the need to align academic research with the ethical tenets of Islām and contribute to developing a comprehensive understanding of Islāmic principles in the context of Islāmic research. It, thus, transcends mere compliance with ethical norms, becoming a dynamic force propelling researchers towards impactful, compassionate, and socially beneficial contributions to the collective welfare of humanity.

7.2.7 Non-maleficence

Non-maleficence, rooted in the Islāmic ethical principle of *al-darar*, is a foundational pillar in guiding researchers towards the conscientious and ethical conduct of studies. Non-maleficence, or *al-darar*, reinforces the prohibition of causing harm, stressing the importance of conducting research that does not inflict physical or psychological distress. Islāmic research ethics requires researchers to minimise risks and ensure the safety and well-being of participants throughout the research process. This includes conducting thorough risk assessments, implementing appropriate safeguards, and monitoring participants' welfare. This goes beyond the physical realm to encompass the psychological, social, and cultural dimensions, where potential harm may not always be immediately apparent.

Considering the potential psychological, social, or cultural harm that may arise, researchers must carefully reassess the worthiness of continuing the research or take steps to mitigate these risks. However, beyond a mere commitment to avoiding harm, non-maleficence encapsulates a proactive responsibility to safeguard the well-being of research participants comprehensively. As such, scholars engaging in research under Islāmic ethical guidelines must implement robust safeguards and remain vigilant throughout the research process, continually monitoring and adapting to the evolving dynamics that could impact participants' welfare. This conscientious approach ensures that the pursuit of knowledge remains morally grounded and socially responsible within the broader framework of Islāmic ethical considerations.

7.2.8 Summary of the Islāmic Ethics on Human Subjects Research

In the Islāmic ethical paradigm, ensuring the well-being of research participants extends beyond the procedural aspects, encompassing the spiritual, psychological, and physical dimensions of their lives. Through the harmonious integration of these ethical principles, Islāmic research not only upholds the sanctity of privacy and confidentiality but also strives for an ethical equilibrium that respects the dignity and rights of all participants. The guidelines highlighted above serve as a comprehensive framework designed to meet the methodological and scientific research standards and, more importantly, uphold the fundamental values of Islām. The framework of Islāmic research ethics emphasises the concept of autonomy, or *al-hurriyyah*, an individual's right to make well-informed decisions, particularly in research participation. It stresses the significance of informed consent, wherein participants are provided with comprehensive information about the research to make voluntary and knowledgeable decisions.

In Islāmic research ethics, obtaining informed consent becomes a nuanced and culturally sensitive process. Researchers are tasked not only with elucidating the intricacies of the research objectives, procedures, and potential risks and benefits but also with a deep awareness of the participants' cultural and religious backgrounds. Informed consent, therefore, becomes an ethical bridge that traverses the realms of research methodology and cultural sensitivity, ensuring that participants, guided by their religious principles, engage in research with a clear understanding and voluntary willingness. This approach acknowledges the diversity within the Islāmic community, recognising that a one-size-fits-all model is insufficient.

Furthermore, Islāmic research ethics underscores the pertinence of keeping participants' information confidential, reflecting the Islāmic value of safeguarding privacy. This harmonious integration of Islāmic values and research ethics that Islāmic research ethics offers reflects a holistic commitment to upholding the dignity and autonomy of individuals within the Islāmic framework. To fortify ethical research practices within an Islāmic framework, researchers can draw upon a rich tapestry of existing guidelines and scholarly works dedicated to Islāmic research ethics. A significant contribution in this realm is the article "Islāmic Psychology: Emergence and Current Challenges" by Naved Iqbal and Rasjid Skinner. This seminal work delves into the intricate interplay between Islāmic ethics and the landscape of psychological research, offering a nuanced understanding of the ethical foundations that underpin scholarly investigations within the Islāmic context. Beyond acknowledging the principles, the authors address the practical challenges when aligning research methodologies with Islāmic ethical norms.

In academic inquiry, the emphasis on adhering to Islāmic ethical principles represents a conscientious effort to integrate moral considerations into every facet of the research process. Beyond a mere acknowledgement of these values, the work underscores their practical application in guiding the selection of research methodologies, the recruitment of participants, and the subsequent data collection and analysis processes. By weaving Islāmic ethical guidelines into the fabric of research practices, scholars contribute to a framework that upholds principles deeply embedded in the Islāmic tradition, fostering an environment of justice, fairness, and respect. This holistic approach enhances the ethical integrity of research and contributes to the broader mission of aligning scholarly pursuits with the timeless values underpinning Islāmic teachings.

7.3 Aligning Psychology Research on Human Subjects with Islāmic Principles: Ethical Dilemmas

Navigating ethical dilemmas in Islāmic human subjects research can be challenging. In the complex landscape of Islāmic human subjects research, researchers face the intricate task of balancing ethical considerations, cultural sensitivities, and the unique demands of their investigations. Researchers may encounter conflicts between ethical guidelines, cultural norms, and the specific requirements of their research. The potential for conflicts between established ethical guidelines and the intricacies of cultural norms underscores the need for a nuanced approach.

Where this is the case, researchers need to seek guidance from authoritative sources such as relevant Islāmic scholars, ethical review boards, and research institutions with expertise in Islāmic ethics. Engaging in ongoing dialogue and consultation with stakeholders and the community being studied can help researchers address these ethical challenges effectively. It fosters transparency and ensures that the research respects and aligns with the values and beliefs of those involved. This proactive engagement is a foundation for ethical decision-making and contributes to developing scientifically rigorous and culturally sensitive research practices. In essence, a comprehensive and collaborative approach is crucial for researchers to address the ethical dilemmas inherent in Islāmic human subjects research responsibly and ethically.

In addition to consulting with relevant stakeholders, researchers can leverage works by authors like Tariq Ramadhan and Dariusch Atighetchi. Works written by these authors and several others contribute to understanding Islāmic research ethics and serve as authoritative guidelines for researchers. *Islāmic Ethics: Sources, Methodology and Application* by Tariq Ramadan explores the ethical principles of Islāmic research and proposes a methodological framework for conducting research within the Islāmic context (Ramadan, 2018). *Islāmic Bioethics: Problems and Perspectives* by Dariusch Atighetchi provides a comprehensive overview of bioethical issues in Islām, including research ethics (Atighetchi, 2007). *Muslim Medical Ethics: From Theory to Practice* by Jonathan E. Brockopp and Thomas Eich offers practical guidance on applying Islāmic ethical principles in health care and medical research (Brockopp & Eich, 2008).

In addition to the aforementioned works, the discourse on Islāmic research ethics extends beyond these texts, encompassing a rich array of scholarly literature that delves into the nuanced intersections of Islām, research, and ethical considerations. Notably, the Islāmic tradition places significant emphasis on ethical conduct, and scholars continue to engage with and interpret these principles in contemporary research endeavours. The intellectual landscape is further enriched by the works of scholars such as Abdulaziz Sachedina, who, in *Islāmic Biomedical Ethics: Principles and Application*, navigates the intricate terrain of biomedical ethics from the Islāmic perspective. Sachedina's work is instrumental in examining the ethical implications of modern medical advancements within the framework of Islāmic teachings, thereby contributing to a more comprehensive understanding of the ethical dimensions inherent in cutting-edge scientific inquiries.

Moreover, the ongoing scholarship in the realm of Islāmic psychology research underscores the dynamic nature of Islāmic research ethics, adapting to the evolving landscape of scientific inquiry while upholding the ethical foundations rooted in Islāmic principles. As researchers grapple with the challenges posed by emerging technologies and ethical dilemmas, the collective body of literature continues to serve as a guiding beacon, offering insights and frameworks that not only navigate the ethical intricacies of research but also foster a deeper appreciation for the symbiotic relationship between Islām and the pursuit of knowledge.

Moreover, Islāmic research ethics, as an evolving field, continues to be explored and developed. The continuous exploration and development of the dynamic landscape of Islāmic research ethics underscores the importance of staying abreast of the latest ethical guidelines and research methodologies. Therefore, researchers must stay informed to ensure that their studies align with Islāmic principles on emerging issues while upholding the rights and welfare of human subjects. As the field evolves, it becomes imperative for scholars to not only adhere to established ethical norms but also actively engage in conversations that shape and redefine these standards, fostering an environment where Islāmic research can flourish ethically and contribute meaningfully to the advancement of knowledge.

7.4 Addressing Bias and Cultural Appropriation

Conducting research within the Islāmic context requires more than methodological rigour; it demands careful consideration of ethical guidelines and avoiding bias, ensuring that the research process respects the cultural nuances inherent in Islāmic psychology. Bias and cultural appropriation are important ethical concerns that researchers in the Islāmic context should address.

7.4.1 Handling Bias

Bias refers to the potential influence of personal, cultural, or religious beliefs on the research process, which may distort findings or compromise the objectivity of the research. Therefore, researchers must engage in reflexivity, which involves critical self-reflection and awareness of oneself. This is crucial because research methodologies are vulnerable to biases, particularly in social sciences and psychology. These biases can arise from a researcher's personal beliefs, values, cultural background, or unconscious prejudices.

Biases can manifest in selecting research questions, sampling methods, data interpretation, and disseminating research findings. Hence, researchers must recognise and actively seek ways to minimise bias at every stage of the research process, from formulating hypotheses to analysing and presenting results to ensure the validity and reliability of study outcomes. Researchers should be self-reflective, digging deep into their biases, assumptions, and the potential impacts on the research process. They should also strive to minimise said biases by maintaining openness, transparency, and intellectual humility throughout the research process (Suleman, 2016).

Another way to minimise biases is to employ multidisciplinary and collaborative research teams. It involves bringing together diverse research teams with varied perspectives and backgrounds. Collaboration fosters dialogue, critical thinking, and mutual accountability. With such diversified backgrounds, research teams can collectively contribute to a more comprehensive understanding of the studied phenomena while helping mitigate individual biases' influence. A third equally effective approach is incorporating rigorous peer review processes and transparent reporting standards. This can serve as an essential safeguard against biased interpretations.

Equally relevant to preventing bias in Islāmic psychology research is the principle of justice, *al-adl*. Islāmic research ethics places great importance on the principle of justice. Justice requires researchers to approach their work with fairness, impartiality, and equity throughout their work, ensuring that all participants are treated with dignity and respect. This commitment to justice makes it imperative for researchers to continuously acknowledge and challenge their biases to maintain integrity and uphold the principle of justice (Ghaly, 2016) Moreover, the concept of justice in Islāmic research ethics is intricately intertwined with the notion of accountability. Researchers are made to understand that they are not only responsible for the scientific rigour of their work but also for ensuring that the human aspects of their research are conducted with the utmost integrity.

7.4.2 Navigating Cultural Appropriation

Cultural appropriation and its ethical implications in the Islāmic research context also demand careful consideration. Cultural appropriation is the unauthorised adoption, borrowing, or misrepresentation of another culture's practices, symbols, or knowledge, often without proper understanding or respect. In Islāmic psychology research, cultural appropriation can occur when researchers extract or use Islāmic concepts, frameworks, or practices without proper understanding or consultation with knowledgeable individuals from the Muslim community. This phenomenon underscores the importance of fostering a more inclusive and collaborative approach to cross-cultural research.

In addition to fostering multidisciplinary and collaborative research teams, preventing cultural appropriation from leaking into research is another crucial aspect of addressing bias in research within an Islāmic framework. Researchers must recognise the potential for misunderstanding, exploitation, or commodification of elements from Islāmic culture and traditions and strive to minimise them. Researchers must ensure their work respects the nuances and sensitivities of the Islāmic culture under study to prevent cultural appropriation. This involves acknowledging the source culture and engaging in respectful dialogue and collaboration with members of that culture, especially those with expertise in Islāmic psychology, to gain a deeper understanding. Moreover, researchers must be vigilant against perpetuating stereotypes or imposing external interpretations on the intricacies of Islāmic beliefs and practices.

Researchers must be sensitive to local customs, traditions, and values, as this sensitivity is crucial to preventing unintentional appropriation and promoting ethical research practices. However, while they are at it, they must avoid allowing these cultures, especially stereotypes within them, to overshadow the reality that Islāmic beliefs genuinely represent. Together, the balance between both, i.e. cultural sensitivity and avoidance of stereotypes, will foster a more inclusive and equitable research environment within the Islāmic context. Upholding this, as a foundational part of Islāmic research ethics, not only promotes the well-being and dignity of research participants but also ensures the integrity and validity of research findings. This collaborative and culturally sensitive approach enriches the research landscape and builds bridges between diverse communities, fostering mutual understanding and respect (Al-Krenawi & Graham, 2000).

An important part of being culturally sensitive is demonstrating a deep understanding of and respecting the religious and cultural context within which research is conducted. This includes consulting with relevant Islāmic scholars, obtaining informed consent from participants, and ensuring that research findings are disseminated accurately and appropriately. Another key part is to avoid sensationalising or misrepresenting Islāmic beliefs, practices, or cultural aspects for personal or academic gain. Cultural sensitivity should extend beyond the initial research design and participant recruitment stages, permeating the entire research process. This involves fostering open and transparent communication with the community, addressing concerns, and adapting research methodologies to align with local customs as the research unfolds. Embracing a collaborative approach involving community members in the research process enriches the study's depth and ensures that findings resonate authentically within the cultural and religious context.

In the realm of research within the Islāmic framework, the imperative task of addressing bias and cultural appropriation extends beyond individual reflexivity to encompass the dynamics of collaborative efforts and the adoption of multidisciplinary approaches. Recognising the inherent complexities of cultural contexts requires researchers to go beyond self-awareness and actively engage with diverse perspectives. Collaborative research teams, with members possessing varied backgrounds and expertise, foster a more nuanced and balanced understanding of the subject matter. This collective approach not only helps mitigate individual biases but also contributes to the richness and depth of the research findings. Furthermore, the ethical navigation of cultural appropriation is vital, emphasising the importance of researchers respectfully approaching Islāmic culture and knowledge. Adhering to established ethical guidelines and drawing upon relevant works on Islāmic research ethics ensures that the research aligns with principles of justice, fairness, and respect, thereby safeguarding the integrity of the research within the context of Islāmic values.

7.5 Conclusion

This chapter has delved into the critical realm of ethical considerations in Islāmic research, emphasising its importance in psychology. It emphasises the importance of methodological considerations in Islāmic psychology research, advocating for rigorous and transparent methodologies aligned with objectivity, validity, and reliability. This chapter extensively explores the ethical foundations of Islāmic research, underscoring the necessity of integrating Islāmic principles and values throughout the research process. The exploration of methodological considerations in Islāmic psychology research highlights the need for a nuanced approach that respects and aligns with Islāmic principles.

The discussion extends to the ethics of human subjects research within the Islāmic context, stressing the need to uphold the principles of justice, beneficence, and respect for autonomy. A noteworthy aspect explored in this chapter is the imperative to address bias and cultural appropriation. Highlighting the need to combat bias and cultural appropriation, this chapter urges researchers to be aware of their biases and engage in meaningful collaborations to combat bias and ensure cultural sensitivity. Furthermore, the discussion on the ethics of human subjects research within the Islāmic context underscores the significance of upholding the dignity and rights of individuals, emphasising the need for informed consent, confidentiality, and cultural sensitivity. Recognising the potential for distortion or misrepresentation, researchers in Islāmic psychology must strive to engage with cultural nuances respectfully and authentically.

This chapter guides researchers in the broader context of research ethics, urging them to navigate the intricate landscape of Islāmic research with a profound awareness of the ethical dimensions involved. As the field of Islāmic psychology continues to evolve, a commitment to ethical principles will bolster the credibility of research and foster a more inclusive and respectful scholarly community. Researchers must reflect on the ethical considerations discussed herein and integrate them into their work, advancing knowledge while upholding the principles of justice, integrity, and cultural sensitivity in Islāmic psychology research.

References

Abū Raiya, H., & Pargament, K. I. (2010). Religiously integrated psychotherapy with Muslim clients: From research to practice. *Professional Psychology: Research and Practice*, *41*(2), 181.

Abū-Rabia, A. (2013). Infertility and surrogacy in Islāmic society: Socio-cultural, psychological, ethical, and religious dilemmas. *The Open Psychology Journal*, *6*(1).

Abū-Raiya, H., & Pargament, K. I. (2015). Religious coping among diverse religions: Commonalities and divergences. *Psychology of Religion and Spirituality*, *7*(1), 24.

Al-Krenawi, A., & Graham, J. R. (2000). Culturally sensitive social work practice with Arab clients in mental health settings. *Health & Social Work*, *25*(1), 9–22.

Ali, A. (1988). Scaling an Islāmic work ethic. *Journal of Social Psychology*, *128*(5), 575. https://doi.org/10.1080/00224545.1988.9922911

Ali, A. J., & Al-Owaihan, A. (2008). Islāmic work ethic: A critical review. *Cross Cultural Management: An International Journal*, *15*(1), 5–19. https://doi.org/10.1108/13527600810848791

Atighetchi, D. (2007). *Islāmic bioethics: Problems and perspectives* (Vol. 31). Springer.

Brockopp, J. E., & Eich, T. (2008). *Muslim medical ethics: From theory to practice*. University of South Carolina Press. https://books.google.com.ng/books?id=Fla1InQ-kjMC

Dasti, R., Farhan, R., Naqvi, T. F., Sitwat, A., & Bokharey, I. Z. (2020). Ethical and moral dilemmas in psychotherapy: Applying a religiously sensitive framework to therapy. In *Working with Muslim clients in the helping professions* (pp. 242–258). IGI Global.

Ghaly, M. (2016). *Islāmic perspectives on the principles of biomedical ethics* (Vol. 1). World Scientific.

Iqbal, N., & Skinner, R. (2021). Islāmic psychology: Emergence and current challenges. *Archive for the Psychology of Religion*, *43*(1), 65–77.

Lee, Y., Lee, M., & Park, S. (2017). Mental health status of North Korean refugees in South Korea and risk and protective factors: A 10-year literature review. *European Journal of Psychotraumatology*, *8*(sup2), 1369833.

Lombardi, C. B. (2005). *Islāmic ethics of life: Abortion, war and euthanasia*. JSTOR.

Ramadan, T. (2018). Islāmic ethics: Sources, methodology and application. In *Islāmic bioethics: Current issues & challenges* (pp. 1–21).

Rassool, G. H. (2023). *Integrated research methodologies in Islāmic psychology*. Taylor & Francis.

Rassool, G. H. (2024). *Islāmic counselling and psychotherapy: An introduction to theory and practice*. Taylor & Francis.

Suleman, M. (2016). Contributions and ambiguities in Islāmic research ethics and research conducted in Muslim contexts: A thematic review of the literature. *Journal of Health & Culture*, *1*(1), 46.

8 Advancing Islāmic Ethics in Islāmic Psychology

8.0 Conclusion

Throughout this journey, we have learned that Islāmic ethics provide a comprehensive framework for understanding human behaviour and promoting psychological well-being. We established that the principles of Islāmic ethics, such as justice, compassion, and responsibility, align closely with many psychology theories and interventions while building upon them. Considering this, we emphasised incorporating Islāmic values and teachings into psychological assessments and interventions. This incorporation is key because psychologists can provide more effective and relevant support by understanding the spiritual dimension of individuals and their unique cultural context. Still, this requires psychologists to have a strong knowledge base of Islāmic ethics and an appreciation for the diversity within the Muslim community.

Furthermore, the exploration of Islāmic ethics in the context of psychology has shed light on the rich and profound insights that Islāmic teachings offer to promote well-being and resolve psychological challenges. We discussed the significance of promoting a balanced approach to mental health in Islāmic psychology. Islām encourages a holistic view of well-being, encompassing the physical, psychological, and spiritual dimensions. Islāmic ethics offers a profound and comprehensive framework for addressing contemporary issues in psychology. Integrating spirituality into therapeutic practices can bridge the gap between religious and psychological perspectives and foster a more profound sense of purpose and meaning, offering individuals a more profound source of resilience and coping while providing a more holistic and culturally sensitive approach to mental health.

But it starts with having a firm understanding of the concept of moral development in Islāmic ethics and its relation to psychological growth. The pursuit of moral excellence is a central tenet of Islāmic ethics. Islāmic psychology cultivates virtues such as patience, gratitude, forgiveness, and humility. Establishing justice and compassion in interpersonal relationships is another crucial aspect of Islāmic ethics. Islāmic psychology recognises the importance of empathy, kindness, and fairness in promoting healthy relationships. These

DOI: 10.4324/9781032658858-11

virtues contribute to individual well-being and foster harmonious relationships and a just society.

In addition to cultivating virtues, Islāmic teachings emphasise the importance of overcoming vices to attain a higher moral consciousness. Psychological interventions rooted in Islāmic ethics can help individuals develop these virtues, enabling them to lead more fulfilling lives and contribute positively to their communities. Psychological interventions informed by Islāmic values can equally guide conflict resolution, communication skills, and emotional regulation, enhancing interpersonal interactions and fostering more substantial, more compassionate communities. By aligning psychological theories and interventions with Islāmic values, we can foster a deeper understanding of human behaviour and promote ethical decision-making. More importantly, with practitioners, patients and researchers all willing to allow their psychology practice, psychological well-being, and mental health research, respectively, to be influenced by a potent combination of mainstream and Islāmic ethical guidelines, the potential for enhancing mental health and well-being, and contributing to psychology research is limitless.

Another key takeaway from the discussions on Islāmic ethics is the centrality of the belief in the oneness of Allāh. This belief is the foundation for understanding the interconnectedness of all aspects of life, including psychological well-being. Recognising this interconnectedness allows individuals to approach psychological challenges from a spiritual perspective, seeking solace and guidance in their faith. Integrating Islāmic teachings and practices into psychological interventions will provide a sense of meaning and purpose, helping individuals navigate their struggles with a stronger sense of resilience and hope. As we continue to explore and advance this field, Islāmic psychology practitioners and researchers must embrace the principles of Islāmic ethics and strive to create a more compassionate, just, and psychologically flourishing society.

Furthermore, cultural sensitivity and context are essential considerations in the practice of Islāmic psychology. Muslims come from diverse cultural backgrounds and may face unique challenges influenced by their cultural contexts. Recognising this diversity and appreciating the various interpretations and cultural contexts in the Islāmic context is crucial. Therefore, psychologists working with Muslim individuals should be aware of and sensitive to these cultural nuances, tailoring interventions accordingly. By integrating Islāmic ethics and cultural sensitivity, psychologists can establish a safe and supportive environment that respects and honours individuals' identities and values. Thus, in the future, cultural competence and sensitivity, now recognised as integral parts of the Islāmic psychology framework, have become essential when working with Muslim individuals, as their beliefs, values, and practices often vary significantly. By embracing this diversity, psychologists can establish a strong therapeutic alliance and create a safe space for clients to explore their concerns within the Islāmic ethical framework.

However, it is essential to recognise that the development of Islāmic psychology is an ongoing process that requires the collective effort of scholars, practitioners, and communities. Consequently, based on the insights gained from this exploration of Islāmic ethics in Islāmic psychology, several recommendations can be made to advance the field and promote well-being among Muslim individuals.

8.1 Recommendations

Education and Training: There is a need for education and training programmes that equip mental health professionals with knowledge and understanding of Islāmic ethics and psychology. This will enable them to provide culturally sensitive and effective interventions for concerned Muslims, addressing their unique needs and concerns.

Collaboration: Encouraging collaboration between Islāmic scholars, psychologists, and other mental health professionals can foster a more integrated approach to addressing psychological challenges within the Muslim community. By bringing together expertise from both Islāmic ethics and psychology, a comprehensive understanding of the individual's well-being can be achieved.

Research: Further research is necessary to explore the effectiveness of interventions rooted in Islāmic ethics. Investigating the impact of spirituality, mindfulness, and virtue cultivation on psychological well-being can contribute to developing evidence-based practices in Islāmic psychology.

Community Engagement: Engaging with Muslim communities and religious leaders is crucial for disseminating knowledge about Islāmic ethics and psychology. By fostering dialogue and collaboration, mental health professionals can build trust and enhance community support for psychological interventions.

Policy and Advocacy: Advocating policies that promote cultural sensitivity and accommodate the unique needs of Muslims in mental health settings is essential. This includes ensuring access to mental health services aligning with Islāmic ethics and addressing barriers.

Other Recommendations: Stakeholders are urged to establish research centres and institutes dedicated to studying Islāmic ethics in psychology. These institutions can facilitate collaborative research, provide resources for scholars and practitioners, and promote interdisciplinary approaches.

Universities and educational institutions are equally encouraged to include courses on Islāmic ethics in their psychology curricula. This will ensure that future psychologists receive comprehensive training that incorporates cultural and religious diversity. Educational institutions should also foster international collaborations and partnerships to exchange knowledge and experiences across countries and regions. This will contribute to the global development of Islāmic ethics in psychology. Conferences, workshops, and symposiums on Islāmic ethics in psychology should also be organised. These events can serve as platforms for networking, sharing research findings, and discussing emerging issues in the field.

Professional organisations in psychology should advocate the inclusion of Islāmic ethics in their organisations' ethical guidelines and professional standards. This will promote ethical conduct and culturally sensitive practice among psychologists. In the same vein, mental health boards should support community-based initiatives that aim to integrate Islāmic ethics in mental health services. This can involve partnering with community-based organisations, mosques, and religious leaders to provide accessible and culturally appropriate psychological support. Adopting these recommendations is critical as advancing Islāmic ethics in Islāmic psychology requires a multidimensional approach that encompasses research, training, collaboration, community engagement, and advocacy.

8.2 Future Directions for Islāmic Ethics in Islāmic Psychology

Several recommendations are worth exploring as we consider the future directions for Islāmic ethics in Islāmic psychology. First, there is a need for further research in the field of Islāmic psychology. While some studies have begun to investigate the integration of Islāmic ethics into psychological practice, more empirical evidence is required to establish the efficacy of these approaches. Research can help validate the impact of Islāmic ethics on mental health outcomes and guide the development of evidence-based interventions. In addition, collaboration and dialogue between Islāmic scholars and psychologists should be encouraged. Scholars can provide valuable insights into Islāmic traditions, interpretations, and ethical dilemmas, while psychologists can contribute their expertise in psychological theories and practices. This collaboration can lead to the development of culturally sensitive and ethically grounded interventions.

Furthermore, it is essential to incorporate Islāmic ethics into the training and education of psychologists. Graduate programmes in psychology should include courses or modules that specifically address integrating Islāmic ethics into psychological practice. This will ensure that future psychologists are equipped with the necessary knowledge and skills to provide culturally sensitive and ethically informed care to Muslim individuals and communities.

To strengthen the foundation of Islāmic ethics in Islāmic psychology, further research is needed to explore the intersections between Islāmic principles and various psychological theories. This includes investigating the compatibility of Islāmic ethics with cognitive-behavioural approaches, humanistic psychology, positive psychology, and other emerging theoretical frameworks.

It is essential to establish ethical guidelines and professional standards that explicitly incorporate Islāmic ethics into the practice of psychology. This can involve collaborations between Islāmic scholars, psychologists, and professional organisations to create a framework that promotes ethical conduct, cultural sensitivity, and integrating Islāmic values in therapeutic settings. Such guidelines can help psychologists navigate ethical dilemmas and ensure their practice aligns with the principles of Islāmic ethics.

To equip psychologists with the necessary knowledge and skills, there is a need for specialised training programmes and educational resources that integrate Islāmic ethics into psychology curricula. This can include courses, workshops, and certification programmes that provide psychologists with a comprehensive understanding of Islāmic ethics and its application in psychological practice. In addition, integrating Islāmic ethics into existing psychology training programmes can help foster culturally competent practitioners who can effectively serve Muslim individuals and communities.

To further advance the field of Islāmic psychology, collaboration between psychologists, Islāmic scholars, and other relevant disciplines is crucial. Interdisciplinary approaches can facilitate the exchange of knowledge, ideas, and perspectives, leading to innovative research, interventions, and policies informed by Islāmic ethics. Collaborative efforts can also promote a holistic understanding of human behaviour, considering individuals' spiritual, psychological, and social dimensions. Furthermore, collaboration with other branches of psychology, such as cross-cultural psychology, positive psychology, and clinical psychology, can enrich the field of Islāmic psychology by integrating diverse perspectives and methodologies.

Community engagement and advocacy are vital in advancing Islāmic ethics in psychology. Psychologists can actively engage with Muslim communities to understand their unique needs, concerns, and experiences. Advocacy efforts can also raise awareness about the importance of integrating Islāmic ethics in psychological practice and promote the recognition of Islāmic psychology as a legitimate and valuable field.

To ensure the growth and visibility of Islāmic ethics in psychology, it is essential to encourage scholars and practitioners to publish their work in reputable journals and disseminate their findings through conferences and other platforms. This will contribute to the body of knowledge and foster dialogue among researchers and practitioners interested in Islāmic ethics and psychology.

8.3 Final Words

As we conclude this chapter, we have summarised the key points discussed throughout our exploration of Islāmic ethics in Islāmic psychology. We have emphasised the importance of integrating Islāmic values into psychological theory, research, and practice while maintaining cultural sensitivity and context. By exploring future directions, such as further research, the development of ethical guidelines, training and education, and interdisciplinary collaboration, we pave the way for the advancement and growth of Islāmic ethics in psychology. With continued dedication and collective effort, Islāmic psychology can offer a holistic and culturally appropriate approach to promoting well-being and flourishing among Muslim individuals and communities.

We have explored the contemporary issues surrounding Islāmic ethics and their relevance in psychology. One of the key takeaways from this exploration is the significance of integrating Islāmic values into psychological theory and research. By acknowledging the central role of religion in the lives of Muslims, psychologists can develop a more comprehensive understanding of human behaviour and mental processes within the Islāmic framework. This integration can lead to the development of more effective interventions that resonate with the values and beliefs of Muslim clients.

Furthermore, we have emphasised the importance of cultural sensitivity in Islāmic psychology. We have also recognised the need for Islāmic psychologists to address the unique challenges faced by Muslim individuals and communities and to provide culturally sensitive and contextually appropriate interventions. It is essential to understand the diverse cultural backgrounds and experiences of Muslim individuals to provide relevant and adequate psychological support. Islāmic psychologists should be attentive to the unique challenges faced by different Muslim communities, such as acculturation issues, discrimination, and identity struggles.

Looking towards the future, it is pertinent to continue advancing Islāmic ethics in psychology. Further research is needed to explore the intersection of Islāmic values and psychological processes and investigate the efficacy of Islāmic-based interventions. In addition, developing ethical guidelines specific to Islāmic psychology is imperative. These guidelines should outline the ethical considerations and best practices for conducting research and providing psychological services within the Islāmic context. This framework can ensure that psychologists uphold the principles of justice, beneficence, and non-maleficence while respecting their clients' religious and cultural values.

To support the growth of Islāmic ethics in psychology, adequate training and education programmes must be established. Universities and training institutes should incorporate Islāmic psychology into their curricula, providing students with the necessary knowledge and skills to work effectively with Muslim clients.

The advancement of Islāmic ethics in Islāmic psychology holds great potential for promoting the well-being and flourishing of Muslim individuals and communities. By integrating Islāmic values into psychological theory, conducting culturally sensitive research, and providing contextually appropriate interventions, psychologists can address the unique challenges faced by Muslims. Through continued dedication, research, development of ethical guidelines, training and education, and interdisciplinary collaboration, Islāmic psychology can offer a holistic and culturally relevant approach to psychological well-being. By embracing this approach, we can strive towards a more inclusive and comprehensive understanding of human behaviour and pave the way for a brighter future for Muslim individuals and communities.

Index

MIX
Papier | Fördert gute Waldnutzung
FSC® C083411

Kolibri 360 GmbH
Ferdinand-Jühlke-Straße 7
99095 Erfurt, Deutschland
produktsicherheit@kolibri360.de